TAYLOR MADE
Life of an Entrepreneur, Mother and Celebrity Event Planner

Liz Taylor

A Wild Wolf Publication

Published by Wild Wolf Publishing in 2021

Copyright © 2021 Liz Taylor

First print

All opinions are the personal opinions of the author.

ISBN: 978-1-907954-78-8
Also available as an e-book

www.wildwolfpublishing.com

This book is dedicated to all the shining stars that inspired me. Especially my two daughters, Goldie and Katie, who were the reason I embarked on a journey that took me beyond my wildest expectations!

Liz Taylor is in the business of making dreams come true. What could be a nightmare if left to you personally without doubt becomes a living fantasy.

She takes the hard work out of what most of us want but have no idea how to achieve. For instance, I had no desire to have a 50th birthday party, but from the moment I met Liz at a Manchester United function she convinced me that I would regret not doing it. I don't know if that would have been the case, but it's hard to say no to Liz and what I do definitely know is that I didn't regret a moment of doing it. I live most of my life in London, have home and all my family circle in Belfast and spend an awful lot of my free time in Manchester, within Old Trafford following United. Elizabeth joined those worlds together for me, convincing me that everyone I knew would naturally gravitate to a football themed celebration at The Theatre of Dreams. And they did. Within our function room, the dance floor became a football pitch, the tables were massive footballs cut in half, the waiting staff were all dressed in United kits and the backdrop of the ground, illuminated at night just for us, became the most magnificent setting for photographs. That memory will be with me and everyone who attended forever. It is a happy memory, an exciting memory, an extravagant memory and one which will always give me something to talk about.

Thank you Liz.

After that huge success it was a no brainer that Liz should organise my wedding to Ruth. It was a given that I liked Liz a lot. We are both quite no-nonsense, but all of that would count for nothing if the bride to be couldn't make the same connection – and they did. Maybe sharing the same birthday as Ruth helped. Though neither of them are Irish, they both share 17 March, the Feast Day of Ireland's patron saint St Patrick.

To hand the most important day of your life as a couple to a complete stranger takes a lot of trust and confidence in that person. Make no mistake, Liz knows what she is doing and that

4

comes across. Not to the extent that it is her way or the highway, but with enthusiasm, great ideas, and yet still being open to the quirks and foibles of The Couple. She knows it is their day, but my goodness me, how in so many ways she took away the stress and added so many laughs along the way. Ours was a marquee wedding on what turned out to be the hottest day of the year. Anticipating a crisis on the morning, Liz was up with the larks bringing in and commandeering from wherever she could portable fans and air con units. Ruth remembers looking out of her hotel bedroom window at 6 am and seeing the normally high-end dressed Liz in a tracksuit assembling her troops, pulling cables, dressing tables and just being there to make sure nothing went wrong. Come the event you don't see her. She is behind the scenes orchestrating, working her magic. All we have to do is enjoy the results.

My relationship with Liz Taylor started out as a business arrangement, but very quickly turned into a friendship for life between her, Ruth and myself. As TV people, we know that watching her at work and play is pure theatre. That is why she has made many appearances on programmes, including our own *This Morning*. Her advice is spot on, no nonsense. She has been there, done it, got the t-shirt. Indeed, looking at her CV we feel quite honoured that she considered working with *us*, bearing in mind who she has as clients and the events and scale she has worked on over the years and around the world. With a name like Elizabeth Taylor you would expect something special, and believe me you get it. She is a whirlwind, a tour de force, an expert in her field, has worked for The Glitterati – and us.

In this book you will find out why she is so special and how she deals with the business of a show business world. So be prepared to meet and get to know the LT in the TLC Corporation...

Prologue

Here I am on holiday. A beautiful room with a magnificent view in a place I feel happy.

I'm on my own. Having arrived last night and unpacked, I'm looking forward to a well-earned break. 2020 into 2021 has been the most challenging in my career, but I've survived. I've done more than survive; I've grown. Two inches taller actually, as I stand with my back straight and head held high.

I put the vibrator back in its bag. Oh my goodness, did I just share that? The taboo subject that only single members dare voice. Well, let me tell you, by the time I opened the box, found my reading glasses, read the instructions, fathomed out the speed and settings, the moment had passed and I spent ten minutes trying to turn the bugger off.

So, I make my way down to breakfast in a rather swanky hotel in Portugal. It's my third visit and I love this place. Since 2016, I have sought solace at a retreat in Turkey and more recently this bolt hole in the Algarve. Places I felt comfortable, convinced that this was an integral part of my recovery programme post-divorce.

A table for one, the waiter asks. I look behind and reply, well, unless you can see someone I can't. I immediately mentally reprimand myself for my unnecessary response as he says, sorry madam, I just wondered if you were joining anyone. Note to self.

I take my seat in the sunshine and order my staple fresh grapefruit juice, two poached eggs on sour dough and peppermint tea. I've done my morning run in the gym and am energised. I look around and observe. Every single family member on a mobile phone. Not communicating, sharing precious time on a tablet. The art of conversation hovering above. I look at the blue sky and watch the palm trees around the pool bow to the morning sun.

As I'm a creature of habit I move from my Table for One and make my way down to the beach. Here, Paulo has reserved my bed. On the front, so I can smell the sea, watch the

6

waves and soak up the sun with the wonderful breeze that works its way along the sand. I take out my headphones. I've listened to every self-help book over the last eight years, convinced that they will be my crutch for recovery. Gabrielle Bernstein, Marie Forleo, Rhonda Byrne, Ekhart Tolle, you name it I've read it. This time I find myself thumbing through podcasts. I can't listen to my own, Events That Made Me – that's narcissistic and I'm just recovering from living with a narcissist. I stumble on Life's a Beach – Alan Carr interviewing the great Sir Tom Jones, Rufus Wainwright, Tom Daly and Amanda Holden, and I decide to join him. I'm instantly addicted. I lie there, hysterical at the ad libs and one liners that float my boat. Before I look round, it's mid-afternoon and I order an ice cold beer. My therapist, who drove my recovery bus, is in the same resort and WhatsApp's me, inviting me to join her for a Mojito. Great – a free session – time to unburden my inner soul. She meets me on the deck an hour later and comments on my wellbeing. Right I think – let's make use of this time. I can't. We discuss her kids, my kids, her grandchildren, my grandchildren, the recovery of my industry that is my aphrodisiac, and after three hours and too many mojitos, it dawns on me. I'm no longer and never will be on a Table for One. I'm back.

1 It's My Party and I'll Cry If I Want To

The *party* starts on 17 March 1956 in Didsbury – a smart, affluent suburb of Manchester. I am named after my paternal grandmother.

Elizabeth Taylor.

It is Manchester Derby Day in town. Dad goes to the match. Priorities set.

Four years later my parents have obviously decided that I was not by that point a car crash and my sister Caroline is born. She doesn't survive. In 1960, my brother Robert arrives. At nursery his teacher suspects he is struggling to hear. These are the dynamics that shaped my childhood.

Dad is a barrister and by the age of 45, a judge. Sometimes there seemed no difference between the court of the law and the justice of home. Unable to give or receive genuine affection, he mistook arrogance and success for protective discipline that manifested itself in bullish behaviour.

Mum played the game. One of five sisters, which then led to eighteen cousins, she simply took on the role of the lawyer's wife – home help a permanent in our house. The ladder to success was firmly secured in our middle class home

Dad was a very unhappy man and yes, it bought you luxury holidays and the chance to see places like Venice or Cannes and cruise destinations around the world before they became mainstream, but it also pays for me to go to private school at the age of four. Sometimes the two were combined. Control was king, much of it was for show and Dad's expectations were sky high for me. And you know what that means. I was only going to disappoint.

'If Elizabeth was not so bossy, she might achieve a lot more,' read an early note on a school report when I was still at that age where most kids were 'polite', 'making progress' and 'coming on well'.

I never embraced any of my education. If you pushed me, I would say maybe English was my favourite. I was always

8

rather eloquent. Nor did I particularly idolise any of the teachers so the connection was blank. No role models there to encourage the wild child to set free. All straight down the line – as you would expect at that price. I was a daughter and a sister but didn't toe the line and my independence was in fact considered insolence and a constant un-nurtured strength.

Coming from a large family with my paternal grandfather a successful self-made property developer, I formed lots of friends from many religions and walks of life. I knew that our Jewish community was our hub but also one where your business was never your own and everyone had a story beginning with 'My father came over here with nothing'! One-upmanship and letting people know your status was rising cut in early. Yet that post-war society bred a hard-working ethic and a survival instinct. If something bad happened on our doorstep, everyone would rally round. So, these are the genes I was handed!

When asked what I wanted for my fourth birthday, I confidently requested 'piano lessons'. I knew I loved music and I suppose it was the first glimpse of what lay ahead.

Later, I would invest serious amounts of money and time on therapy with the sole purpose of trying to understand why I felt a failure.

I don't know where it all came from.

Dad's own childhood was tough – he would go to school, cook dinner, stoke the fire and came from a working class background. His Mum was tough and his father a yes man. Later, his younger brother died at the age of 32. You can see perhaps why the desire to escape drove him.

It was all about status. If he wanted the first Citroen in the U.K., so buy the first Citroen. We move to affluent Hale in Cheshire when I was eleven and are only the third Jewish family to do so. To all intents and purposes, we had an enviable lifestyle.

The stability came through family. The *tradition* of religion over its sentiment was the glue, the safety net and sense of belonging. I liked that and to this day, still always prepare a Friday night dinner for the family.

Of course, I felt rejection.

Obviously, I craved attention.
Do I have any happy memories of growing up?
Only now am I beginning to find them.

2 You're Just Like Your Father

By the time I was almost legal to do legal things I was more than ready to break free. Pretty much brought up as an only child with Robert being sent away for schooling, it was only a matter of time before I cut loose.

That meant I never made A Levels. I knew I would fail anyway through disinterest.

At the age of seventeen in that first year of sixth form, everything changed. My parents' marriage was falling over. Dad left us in Greece and just came home early. He was having an affair and that was that. Gone.

So while my parents were pre-occupied, I became free. I already had a Saturday job at *Emma Somerset,* a privately owned ladies fashion boutique in Manchester.

The shackles were off. I didn't respect the family scenario and I knew I had to make my own money. Just like my Dad, that insecurity over cash meant that I started earning as soon as I could, and dreamt big – and with no thought towards the consequences of my actions.

Dad was very intrusive with no respect for anything private. I had kept a five year diary, which he routinely read. I was floundering through adolescence. I had already discovered nightclubs trying hard to cover my tracks but perhaps wanting to be caught too. Dad defending George Best was just an excuse for me to go to his club Blinkers. I was one step ahead attracting the attention I craved. The bursts of insincere concern just added fuel to my fire – Dad's punishments almost Dickensian.

From fourteen, chauffeurs had been regularly picking up my girlfriends and I and dropping us at the Jewish Club in Manchester. I would put on my high heels en route with no fear or awareness for personal safety. Dad always thought the worst, never understanding that mutual trust and respect and hitting me for the first time on an assumption that was just a figment of his imagination.

I just wanted to have fun and didn't feel I was rebelling, though of course I see that now. I just thought I was finding my feet. What I earned, I would then spend on make up, forced to hide it from Dad. The rest would go on fags. There was always a curfew and always a drama.

I lived for Saturdays.

My relationship with my brother was different. Dad mollycoddled him a lot because of his hearing, I mothered him a fair bit too – albeit only really in the school holidays as he boarded away. We were very close and he saw a lot, as I did – Dad being very verbally and physically abusive and a lot of bullying.

Beyond that, we had little in common. He had only ever known being looked after and I only wanted to look away. By the time, the real world kicked in for Robert, he wanted to be an osteopath and met a Canadian in the process, moving there, marrying there and then staying there after divorce.

When Dad died in 2006, only I went to see him. In his hour of need, the mask came off confessing that he regretted everything and told Mum so too. By then, he also had a further two wives, having done the unthinkable in marrying the spouse of a client and then inheriting two children. He went on to bully his second wife's eldest. After that came the mother of a friend of mine whom he stayed with for 24 years – much of that was toxic too. He barely saw his grandchildren. Hugely successful on the exterior, the inside wanted its time again, unable to have or sustain a loving relationship.

At his funeral, I remember shivering when the car arrived then crying uncontrollably at what I had missed out on – less tearful for the man, more so for the void. Sometime after and symbolic of his unpredictability in an attempt to get *my* attention, the door rang one night at my home in Hale, Cheshire and someone had left a parcel. Inside were photographs.

All of them were of me from birth, tied and wrapped in brown paper – an attempt to remove me from his life.

Then there had been the suicide note posted previously in an attempt to remove himself from his life. I shrugged when I got it in the knowledge that he was too cowardly to take his own life.

And yet, over the years, I have frequently been told that 'you're just like your father' – few expressed it as a compliment. Therapy has taught me that he did mean something to me. For him and I it was too late but I have made my peace and used it as a tool to help me going forward in how you, yourself, deal with people.

We *could* have been very close whereas he actually left a huge hole. When I reflect I know that I am a success because of him yet I can't see him anywhere when I replay in my mind the key scenes in my life. Intellectually, I know we were of the same ilk but he never showed me an awareness of that. I *heard* that he was proud of what I went to achieve but crucially, I didn't know that from him.

Of course, this leads to promiscuity at fourteen and several failed marriages of my own. It made it hard for me to settle down but did make me a better mother. I remain very close to *my* Mum now but she struggled to be that person to me *because* of Dad, which I also now understand. She was not challenging to him whereas he lived for every conquest.

Home life to me literally went out of fashion.

I loved selling and I knew that I was good at it. Confidence came quickly. This is often still mistaken for arrogance…and now suddenly, at Emma Somerset, I was in the fashion business.

Instantly, my patter became a challenge to the older ladies working there on commission. I was starting to take a piece of their pie. Pocket money represented control from Dad. I wanted my own cash. Unsurprisingly, the fashion business met with disapproving eyes too. Today, I sometimes wish that I had been a lawyer like Dad but the fact of the matter is that when I was eight, I was already heading off to fashionable Wilmslow in Cheshire and buying black pinafores without hesitation. He was appalled at my confidence and that fashion statement of course showed that I was beginning to express myself. To make matters worse, the voice of anarchy was also writing songs, though with no great success and got my first holiday without parents out of the way at sixteen whilst managing to cover my tracks. Thankfully, Dad didn't rent a villa in the same resort!

Mum had re-married and gone to live with her new partner. I moved in to my own flat. Self-sufficiency is now key.

At eighteen, Marks and Spencer were advertising for applicants to get on their much-acclaimed managerial course. This was not far off the equivalent of a degree and pretty tough to be selected for. I knew I could get an interview with all my admin and organisational skills. I worked out too that I couldn't make management if I didn't learn to do *everyone's* job.

Therein lies a standard to which I am true today.

I was in, and based just a mile away in Altrincham but knowing that they could send you wherever they wanted whenever they wanted just to test you. I knew this would not be good enough for Dad but it felt very liberating. Financially, I was going to be fine and I was starting to meet people from all sorts of walks of life and learning everything to make the management grade. It ticked all the boxes.

However, even though I had been living fairly streetwise for most of my teen years, I really wasn't emotionally mature enough to start touring the country, and after eighteen months they worked out after clocking my mileage that instead of living near the store they had sent me to as I was supposed to, I had in fact been commuting from Cheshire. On my terms – even then!

As a punishment, to test my commitment, they instructed me to move to Glasgow. I left there and then. I was not being told. And certainly not being told to go to Glasgow.

So, great foundation that it was, I chucked it all away and began working for *Top Shop* and *Top Man*.

I am now 20 and am introduced to the son of a friend of my parents.

We meet in the October. He tells me that he is going skiing with his pals at Christmas. I say fine as long as we get married in March.

So we did.

The fact that I can sum that period of my life up in five sentences…well, frankly, just about says it all.

Crazy, I know – but that is the pace of life I was living at and the speed with which I was charging away from a broken home life. Obviously, Dad didn't approve and told me he wasn't coming to the wedding leaving me traumatised on the day uncertain if he would show.

But he did show up and ruined the magic as I made my first trip down the aisle. Everything was a test. Each action met with a disapproval rating. And then it became a statement – a massive synagogue wedding and everything you would expect from a middle class Jewish girl with a tea dance at The Midland Hotel in Manchester.

'Are you sure about this?' Mum asked.

'Yes,' I replied.

I knew I wasn't at all.

On reflection, I should have acknowledged the maternal instincts I now pride myself in.

From the honeymoon, it went downhill fast. Our friends were his friends and I inherited the mother-in-law from hell – controlling, possessive and spoon-feeding him. I understand now that I wanted that sense of tradition on the day rather than it being of any other value and I realise too that I craved a home life and the package rather than the individual. And I wanted to spell it out to my parents that I was now in charge.

Big ideas. Grand statements.

One Monday, I called a friend who was single having split young from her marriage.

'Can I come and stay for a few weeks?' I asked.

She agreed.

So, just one month after moving from our Liverpool flat to a gorgeous cottage in the suburb of Aigburth and eighteen into our marriage, I packed my things and left the following note:

'Dinner is in the oven. The dog has been fed. I've left.'

And I was gone.

And he never sought to find me.

I returned only briefly to take my share from all the wedding gifts he had laid out for me to pick from. I had ignored the lipstick I had found on a glass when we had been at the flat and we were both as glad as each other to see the back of one another. His parents were not best pleased; mine found it inevitable. I was waiting for I told you so. I was wild and vulnerable and see now how irresponsible it was.

I have no regrets.

It shapes you.

Next stop Manchester. No crocodile tears.

No crocodile tears, just an opportunity with the high-end brand of the same name. Crocodile. I am introduced to Peter Davies and begin running their Manchester store. For three weeks, I am back and forth between London and Manchester as Area Manager. I am a little bit of naughty girl in the capital breaking free from my marriage but my eyes are opened to London and Bond Street in particular.

I liked the whole mentality of importing from Hong Kong and then escalating the prices at home. Entrepreneur was the way to go.

Around 1980, the high street begins to thrive around Manchester through brands like Kendals and the Royal Exchange and the renowned Arndale Centre. I see opportunity. Gut feeling is a big thing for me rather than pursuing any kind of plan and my instinct was that this was the place to be, making money, using my social skills, meeting great people and without realising its impact in the moment, but beginning to create my little black book of contacts.

Life was on the up.

Then I met husband number two in a bar.

You can shout 'slow down, Liz' all you like but I only know one pace and this is it.

Michael was a fun, well-educated Jewish accountant. You can guess the next bit. From the off, Dad was against it even though I had actually known Michael for some time before we got together. By August 1983, we were married.

I thought it was expected of me. This was the course to take. This time, Dad, it is for real. There was no attraction – I believed marriage was friendship and that he would father my children and look after me. It was his second time around too but he also had two young daughters who had moved to New York. When you are young and in the moment, that is where you are. That does not mean caught up in a tidal wave of passion and love – far from it but somehow as some sort of rejection to what

17

I perceived as my disastrous home life as a child, I seemed hell bent on fast-tracking myself there as an adult. How on earth had I shaped such low expectation for the future when everywhere else I had such big plans? The juxtaposition of my business brain and disconnected heart had begun to take shape.

The day after our honeymoon, I found out why Dad was so set against it. I was made aware of a letter from the Institute of Chartered Accountants. He had embezzled around £250,000 of a client's money.

His parents had paid the debt back but Dad's warnings had fallen on deaf ears. He had at least done the one thing which all parents must at some point – allow their children to make their own mistakes. This however was a colossal one. The following February, he was struck off on the day I discovered I was pregnant.

In November 1984, my first child Goldie was born. Michael's mother, to whom he was devoted, died two weeks previously unable to cope with the shame and stress of it all.

Goldie was named after her Grandma Golda.

Somehow we plough on and produce Katie sixteen months later in 1986.

In 1985, realising that there is no future. I pack our bags with nanny in tow and a fledgling business on the horizon, penniless except for the equity to purchase a small three-bedroomed semi in upmarket Hale Barns.

I'm off.

Some eight years later, the trust fund set up for the children's education is emptied and Michael goes missing, eventually found in North Carolina.

I didn't really know the man at all. Volatile at times, he left me desperately unhappy. It's one of the few times that I should have listened to Dad.

But, I wouldn't have, of course.

The future is bleak.

I have two young children to feed. I have no job and no money in the bank. I need to pull a rabbit out of the hat.

'You should do this for a living, you're so organised,' a very good friend remarked.

And so it began.

It cost me our friendship but this is where I get the party started.

Michael is gone. Needs must.

I get lucky. You make your own luck.

I am asked by a friend to help create a Disney themed Bar Mitzvah at the Radisson Hotel in Manchester. She is going away for Christmas. She tells me to get out of it any publicity that I can and to see what happens.

I never ever work to such vague parameters again.

From this moment on, I am mindful how not to do business with friends:

On the train I meet the guys designing the Granada Studios Tours in Manchester and tell them my plan. They have just rebuilt Baker Street and on the back of it opened up a themed bar. They set to work building a *Cinderella* castle *inside* the Radisson Hotel. This is the Eighties. Nobody has done this in the UK. In time, I gain every referral for anyone who hires their venue for a private event. It is the beginning of a beautiful friendship.

I start to consider building this network and upselling services such as, flowers, tables, chairs, sound and…catering. These are all the ingredients that you need to put on an event but as I start out I am working one by one booking people in without realising it will extend beyond a solitary party. I am that green however that I do not even consider elements such as insurance. If that castle falls on somebody's head, you might as well behead me at its tower. I am pulling together pieces of a jigsaw I know nothing about. They will become my foundations. As would soon become my trademark, I would say yes then work out the how afterwards.

The Bar Mitzvah bat is something that is on the lips of every Jewish parent from birth. You go to many. My friend who asked me to help was a very successful stylish woman wanted to make a statement too. It was not just in my roots.

She was the director. I would play producer. Essentially, I was hiding behind her. She was excited to invest in the unknown. That was the only place I was heading. At this stage, I can tolerate playing second fiddle. I concluded quickly that Bar Mitzvahs were a line of work that would keep on coming and equally if you did a good job once, the family might need you again.

And we did a great job together. Manchester had never seen anything like it nor had the hotel or any of the families attending. Unfortunately, and this is where I learn my first lesson, the *Manchester Evening News* on that occasion wrote a less than flattering piece.

My friend calls me during her break, angry at the article. We almost never speak again. Get whatever publicity you can out of it didn't quite mean that.

However, my phone began to ring and then a little more and whatever damage that article might have been perceived to have caused it showed I offered a service. I was up and running.

The problem was that I had never contemplated juggling a full time job with the kids and events took time to organise and would involve unsociable hours. I would have to go at it hard, but I needed income and that meant I had to get help.

The young Scottish nanny who moved with me ended up staying for a decade. I got my little black book out with a few numbers in it and started calling a few people. A little bit of marketing work and fashion PR paid the bills. But, these were very unsettling times – life was all nappies and bottles and I had little support from my ex. I took the sense of being a parent very seriously.

I got wind that the Holiday Inn chain were selling the Midland Hotel in Manchester. The hotel was floundering. Yeah – my first wedding probably put them out of business!

In my new field, they were understaffed and inexperienced but they had a budget to re-launch – something of

20

a rarity back then. This is one of Manchester's most iconic buildings, standing since 1903 and the birthplace of Rolls Royce when Charles Rolls met Henry Royce and the two went into business together. I engineer a 'chance meeting' with the Director of Sales at The Midland, head into town for an 8 am start, picking up an outfit on the way and before I know it I am being offered the opening night party which is to be a Hollywood Nights theme.

'I'll do it,' I say even though I only really had *Cinderella* on my CV at this point.

I put £200 in the bank, negotiate a fee and I am underway. This is different from a Bar Mitzvah but I still have no real concept of all the elements that you need to source to pull something like this off.

Not only am I borderline clueless as how to proceed, the industry is so raw that I am almost exclusively *it*. The staff at The Midland does not really have a sense yet of what is possible. There is no such thing yet as award ceremonies, staff dos and themed events – certainly not on this scale.

I invented the party!

The Hollywood Night is set.

I begin inviting everyone I can and start raising awareness to PAs in important companies across the city. You have to get past the gatekeeper and that meant the Personal Assistant. In time, such characters would play a key role in getting me work as they reacted to what their own competition was doing. They did more than type up memos and organise diaries. They had the boss's ear and were always one click away from putting you through or cutting you dead. They become the next vital cog in my wheel.

If one insurance company was putting on a show for their staff, another would be charged with bettering it. That would fall on the PA's remit. But they obviously did not know how to put on a show either so I knew that I could radiate that confidence and I was clear that two elements would get you respect – creativity and the ability to take the responsibility away from people who suddenly got asked to throw a party. It takes time of course to build that relationship but I did learn this fast.

21

When people started walking into my events, they were always pleased to see you. It was not as though you were there collecting a debt off them. In 1988, I was the only person in the market. I needed these people in the North West.

For the launch, I secured the services of Chester Harriott – the father of the TV chef Ainsley – who was a very talented singer and pianist working in Manchester. Then I decided to fill the pool with balloons.

Hot on the heels, the Midland tell me that they would now like to do a Circus Night in the September and that RBS have been on asking what all the fuss was about. Rather than just book commercials on TV and radio, they are looking at more creative ways of networking and attracting new business. They want to talk. They are one of the first to be ahead of the game.

I am now in business. But am I?

I am nervous, constantly with that permanent knot in your stomach that all self-employed people know. Do I make a brochure? It's hard to do on two fronts. Nobody really believes at this point that it is an industry and I can't really explain how it is going to work. It is in my head. That is a problem in the early days. I have to persuade people to trust me. They have to buy into me the person because the product is something that they cannot see.

I teach myself a key lesson, which still rings true today. Invest to better yourself. I take myself off to Houston, Texas with fellow event planners, Banana Split – just to observe and learn. Just like some of the businesses starting to look at hiring me, I don't really have a budget for this but I know it is important. America is always bigger and brasher and if I am new to this game, barely in its infancy in this country, then my gut is that there will have been people in the States doing it a whole lot longer and better.

I am overwhelmed by what I see. I am inspired and it makes me believe anything is possible – plus I also nick a few ideas and put them in my back pocket. One day, the opportunity will come to replicate them or do them my way.

Never mind my enchanted palace, I learn of the Waldorf Hotel in New York being turned into a golf course. The how becomes the turn on. *How* have they managed to do this? I am reeled in as though a client myself. I know people back home will be sceptical and think nobody could pull that off. It installs in me the mantra that anything is possible and I must sell my wares of that infectious wonder and curiosity that hits me over The Waldorf. That was the challenge and that was how high the bar was now set. The only problem was, that back in the UK, I was to my knowledge the only person who could see that.

But I knew one thing – you didn't *get* lucky. You made your own luck. So, when the Manchester Chamber of Commerce invited me to go on their stand at a big expo in the same year, I knew to accept without knowing whom I might run into. I learn too not to assume.

A rather *unassuming* lady came by – Julie Cripps didn't seem glamorous or have the wow factor – *but* when we got chatting she *did* have the purse strings to British Gas.

I then went on to work for them for ten years!

With every conversation, I know I am getting better at it. You tick off the mistakes you have already made and know that you won't go there again. Your self-worth – so absent from childhood – rises and with that so do your prices. I am much more confident about the Circus Night with simple touches, creating red and yellow balloons over the tables. I love it and I love that people love it. The Circus Night is there to entertain the clients of The Midland. I see nothing but potential clients for me – all 150 of them. I know already from RBS asking for me that one event is more than one potential referral. I am all over it. I realise that the easiest way to make money is to take commissions on the people I am using. The business begins to establish its dimensions.

I start to work out of what eventually became my downstairs toilet at the back of my utility room! This is now my office. Determination and gut feeling are my weapons. Every day I would set out to meet somebody new. I was juggling of course but these were tough yet very positive times. I was fulfilled and independent. I had almost no time for anything else. Men were out the window. I had to support the girls and was the only one doing so. I needed to remain focussed on growing the business. I couldn't stop once I had started and I didn't dare. My only vision was to continue No dream client list, not yet re-building The Waldorf – just keep working and feed the girls.

Suddenly I look up and five years have passed before I could say that I was *starting* to establish myself in Manchester. It took about three of those before I felt confident enough to move the office from the bog to the moss – Moss Lane in Hale. This was a massive step as well as a new financial commitment but I understood the value of getting dressed to go to work every day. Even if I was sitting in an empty office, I knew in my black suit and Prada handbag that people would notice me.

I wanted that to be part of my act – people to see me as someone who commanded professional respect but was also the girl about town.

By 1991 however, that girl about town was heading for the city.

Had I gone as far as I could go? Absolutely not. Did I think that at the time? Possibly. Something – which reflects a naivety and lingering self-doubt took hold. It stems from that money gene that my Dad and I share – the fear that you would never have enough. He came from little so wanted more. I had plenty on a plate as a child but had that fear that it would go. The more successful I got, the worse that would feel. In 1991, I decided I wanted a salary.

My insecurity in the business peaks here. It was a landmark moment. I was not sure of myself despite the fact that I was turning what I do into a success. I also wanted rid of responsibility. I do understand these thoughts with hindsight and I realise too that it wasn't just about the burden and the bucks. For the first time, I began to work with someone who creatively was ahead of the game and ahead of the one I had invented in Manchester.

Perhaps the feeling that another person was in the game fed the insecurity over money or maybe that fear was always there and I just didn't know at the time that I needed to go to the next level creatively.

Enter Lorraine and Jonathan from the Jonathan Seaward Organisation. They had all the London florists and caterers sewn up – Jonathan had started as DJ and built the business on from there. He was a much bigger fish than that.

His wife had an incredible eye for detail. I wanted to get into London. They had access to different people. He wanted the Jewish market. They would pay me a consistent salary and some profits from the business. It looked like a match made in Heaven.

Here was somebody a skip ahead of me.

We were working on a huge Bar Mitzvah in Manchester with lunch in the synagogue hall. She transformed the synagogue hall into an enchanted forest creating split level dining with Italian balustrades.

Everything was on a bigger scale.

And I mean bigger.

I had got to the stage where I needed to better myself and the only way to do it was to learn again from someone new.

But I also was beginning to take the yes to the Manchester scene. That ultimately would be the key to my future independence and that meant within our relationship, I had to keep a little aside for me.

In The Midland Hotel where it all started, I was struggling with one client for whom I was supposed to be organising a Christmas party. It was heavy going and the traditional gatekeeper to the playmaker was resorting to type. She was a PA where P stood for pain and A for arse.

I tried a different approach – humour.

I had been getting nowhere.

So, I started pinging off dry messages away from my usual blunt, forthright tone, which was shaping my reputation and no word of a lie, the next thing I am in the Isle of Man.

'Meet me at Liverpool Airport at 11 am on Sunday,' came the instruction.

I am guessing something had connected. Here was a personal assistant sifting through thousands of mundane pieces of paperwork (as it was then) every single day and somehow I cut through.

As you can see, I did more than that, arriving on Merseyside in a brand new black Italian suit and full on Liz with designer handbag, flying to I don't know where with I don't know whom.

Then I meet him.

He is, at the time, owner of the Trafford Centre and Peel Holdings. He resides on the *Sunday Times* Rich List. Local publications call him one of the most influential businessmen in the North West.

John Whittaker just walked into my life.

The PA is in tow. He is not even looking me in the eye past the opening 'Good morning'. Whittaker grunts, sauntering through Liverpool Airport moaning about the chewing gum as if he owns it.

I have done my research.

He does.

When we land we pass a colossal mansion and I am thinking 'different league'. Of course, I knew this already but there are different leagues and different leagues. It turns out that estate was on his estate!

When the Rolls Royce pulls up at his home it looms larger than the Vatican with a more impressive ceiling. No offence, Michelangelo.

He shows me round including the huge Mausoleum where his parents are buried. That is the one bit of the tour I remember to this day. I sense trust is being cemented. I connect with his pride and start to understand what is important to him.

Noted. Understand people in a business context. Do your research. Then, really tune in when they take you inside the perimeter wall to what is personal to them.

What followed may have been less easy to recall but I keep my wits as the Bollinger flows. Lunch is served.

And for hosts like John, that can be an occasion in itself. Pork pies, prawn sandwiches and Champagne a plenty – *Ab Fab*'s Patsy would have called it the bare minimum. I am sure it was a continuation of the process in vetting me but everybody in his day to day world seems to attend – the driver, the gardener and of course, the PA! It makes sense. These are the people who see him at all ends of the day and with his guard up and guard down. They are trusted.

I find myself eating ham. This is a big deal. And I say that referring to both the client and religion. I back myself to pull it off and that God will forgive me! I am in complete Liz mode, observing whilst socialising, showing steel but displaying humour and radiating warmth. Drinking water of course. Only water!

The dog cinches the deal.

It leaps up and jumps on me, moulting over my Piazza Sempiani suit, nestling for an afternoon nap.

'My dog never has never taken to anyone like that,' John opens up.

I know I am in and we are about to talk numbers.

My heart is in my mouth. How am I going to negotiate with this guy?

He can have whatever he wants and is probably used to getting his own way, and unlike many of us, has the power to walk away from a deal.

Except, I have made it to this stage and I am the only one here.

'What is it going to cost me?' he finally asks.

'I will work for a fee and revoke my commissions,' I blurt, alluding to the financial structure of how I worked.

I go in with a figure. He responds with five grand less.

'It's not negotiable,' I front up.

You have nothing to lose in these moments, but they don't half hang in the air as you find yourself delivering the price.

You've seen those huge pauses on TV quiz and talent shows where they wait an eternity to deliver the verdict. Nobody had a commercial break to cut to. Well, that's how it feels. That's how it *feels* but the reality is that he came straight back.

'You got a deal,' he confirmed.

I am stunned. Trying not to show it, obviously.

Delighted – can't radiate that either.

Keep cool.

I want this man. He has treated me with respect and I will not let him down.

The task ahead – a joint 18th for his son and his own 50th. For the good and the great. No pressure. And no idea how at this point.

We make sculptures out of ice, build into his Italian garden and hang trapeze artists from the bridge which we build over the pond. I build a split level area with a mirrored floor, and fly my band in over from Paris.

This is on another scale. This is off the scale.

What could possibly go wrong?

Answer – almost everything. But it is how you deal with and what you conceal. The show must go on.

My band get stranded in Manchester Airport and by the skin of their teeth make the last plane in. Pause for a moment and think about that. This is a big band, with specialist

28

equipment – not the kind you take as carry on luggage with Ryanair. Not only is it a people logistic, their kit is as vital. One does not come without the other. Except – that is just what happened.

Solved.

Then, once we are up and running my mirrored floor starts moving. Not only is this dangerous, it makes me look rubbish if people realise. I stand to fail. You cannot have people walk away and say that you didn't live up to your promises. You have to improvise. I tell John he has to make his speech now and to make it good and make it long – and of course, I give him no notice.

We usher guests to the upper level and light the candles on the birthday cake.

I send three of my crew underneath the marquee. The supporting wood has shifted. They set to work knowing they are on borrowed time without knowing how long that is. They work miracles. Health and safety is restored. John's speech diverts the guests and they are none the wiser.

I have worked for him ever since.

In 1994, we got the call from an Indian client whose daughter was getting married. Four women turned up at my office in Hale.

I sat opposite them as they talked a language I really couldn't understand.

'What the hell have we got here?' I thought.

'Will you go to Newcastle?' they asked.

'If you send me the airline ticket,' I replied.

I always found a way of radiating that firm self-worth early on. It raised the stakes. If you want me there, get me there properly. Get it right from the off. They came with money and plenty of it but I needed them to know I was on their level.

So I flew to the North East in the days when you still could from Manchester. I am met by a fleet of Mercs to take me to a massive detached house in Jesmond, the most affluent part of Newcastle. In fact, the house is that big I think it is Jesmond. Maybe now, I understand this opportunity.

Deep down, I know it is the Prada handbag that sold it to them.

'This is something else,' I thought. 'This could be an opportunity and a half.'

Of course *that* means cash but it also means I can hang my reputation on this.

Before you build the reputation though you have to build the marquee. 1500 would attend the ceremony. They were hiring the municipal park and that meant closing it for a fortnight. Oh, and I needed hundreds of toilets. I was severely out of my depth without a clue what I was doing. Obviously I go along with the whole thing.

I need to secure a caterer who can handle this head count so I set off to Liverpool to see Paul Feather with his pony tail and diamond in one ear look. Then the two of us return to the main retail park in Newcastle to meet the father – he who pays.

He asks Paul to leave.

'I am going to ask you to organise the wedding,' he announces.

Thank bloody God for that.

'What do you need?'

'20,000 deposit,' I bullshitted. 'Not rupees, pounds.'

I didn't have a clue and nor did he.

'Can we negotiate?' he responded.

'We can negotiate but that is the price!' I answered firmly.

Humour wins.

We shook hands and the deal was done. I grasped that cheque as though my life depended on it. The flight back was so turbulent even the air hostess was sick. I soon discovered that a cheque for 20 Grand is also an excellent fan when needs must.

Now the real arse-wobbling began.

We build a 60 foot by 40 foot kitchen.

Then on the day of the wedding, I have to check my eyes – not because they are watering from the spicy food but because about 20 vans rolled up and Paul hadn't employed any chefs. Instead they unloaded thousands of sealed cartons. I had carefully masterminded this kitchen set up to make everything work smoothly and here we have the biggest take out in history.

Oh – and we are 300 chairs short.

The Indian community – I learn – bring their family along irrespective of the invite!

But when you only realise that as the groom rides into the ceremony on a white horse to be welcomed by everyone, you can't allow yourself to show anything other than control.

Moral of the story?

Always do an Indian wedding. If they tell you it is 1500, add another 300 every time. Plus, make you sure whack 10% on the budget too because while the headcount goes up, their budget goes down! Noted. It is a negotiating tool. They know, you know. Everyone is happy.

You can only laugh sometimes at your naivety.

The bill exceeded £250,000. Monte Carlo or bust. That is why that whatever else is going on, you have got to keep calm and carry on which is why at one point I even ended up cleaning toilets. Pardon the pun but when the shit hits the fan, you will find me there cleaning it! It turns out that the client was the largest importer of ladies clothing into the UK and eventually sold out for £150,000,000.

They would come calling again too and that meant only one thing – next time it would have to be better nor could I make the same mistakes.

Unfortunately, life would make them for me.

Just days before the second daughter was to marry, my specialist feather factory in South Africa blew up in a ball of flames. You might well ask yourself why the hell I needed to go all the way over there to import feathers but that was what we did. Only the best and only the biggest and with the kind of money these people were spending, it made little odds to them. They only wanted to see the result.

Except, I now had 150 tables and none of my specially made orange and purple decorations!

'The feather factory has burnt down,' my partner Dianne was on the phone crying to me. This was by far the biggest wedding we had undertaken at this point. We were about to fail spectacularly.

31

'How many are in the warehouse?' I asked back optimistically.

'About a dozen,' she replied.

My brain was ticking.

'Get the van and drive to Holland,' I told her.

It was mad but seemed logical too.

'Get every orange and purple flower you can. Clear the Dutch out of flowers!'

The race was on.

You had to do what you had to do and to this day, four weddings, a golden wedding and all their children's parties too, the client didn't notice and doesn't know!

I have learnt that it is never worth panicking. The lights can blind them once the event begins but equally you have more hours and resource in the day than you had legislated for if everything goes to plan.

I was very well aware by now that anything rarely did.

Bigger budgets meant these were now bigger benchmarks. Word was spreading and reputation going through the roof. It created a competitive edge amongst potential clients and an almost whispering effect passed your name on.

Many people who booked me once, booked me twice and three times more. And timing sometimes had a lot to do with it.

But I wasn't happy.

I took £26,000 a year in salary and never saw any of the promised bonuses. I brought them in over a million and a half. I learned countless lessons – good and bad.

Lorraine's excellence, which we fed off mutually, never left me. Balloons were naff and out, enchanted forests were in. And it was a lot of fun. They were the positives. But, I was rarely allowed to make any decisions and that was a massive part of who I was. That control which my father exerted over me also passed down. I was a one-man band creating huge events until now. I had to have control.

I had craved that security and was inspired by Lorraine's brilliance but I knew way before it ended that I could never work for somebody else again. And I did actually have a choice. I was only now starting to see it clearly.

Of course, by the end these big issues almost become a sideshow because you start to get distracted by the little irritations. This became more than apparent when they refused to put through a parking ticket on my expenses and I realised that it was time to say 'fuck this'.

So, I did.

Despite my frustrations and that extra element added to the business of trips to London and now being answerable to two other people, this was a period of relative stability. If I went into for a salary and to expand my contacts then it worked.

Perhaps against that backdrop, I was ready to give men another go.

I met Roger in 1993.

I am still dealing with the consequences of it today.

By 1995, we were married. I knew that I had to start to get the work life balance right. Part of that was impossible because I had always played the role of both parents. But after a first marriage which barely counted and a second where I cared about the friendship but *felt* I should marry, now it seemed like this was it. My concerns had only ever been about financial survival and getting the girls educated – and that was costing me ten to £15,000 a year. I had made the mistake of thinking their Dad was responsible as he was a chartered accountant and that turned out to be a colossal error. Now, I had a financial safety net of another account, my kids were not too damaged and it really was time to play happy families.

Roger was to play a key part in my decision making about what to do next. In short, that meant carry on with the clients that I was allowed to keep following the divorce from the Seawards. I knew that they wouldn't really get further into the North West without me and that I had the connections and was now relatively well known. But, lessons learned, I needed my own business *and* did want a partner.

Dianne Lynn was one of my floristry suppliers and became part of the process because I had spent a lot of time confiding in her about my wish to go back on my own. She could see the potential with total clarity and yet, for all my exterior confidence, these two decisions – wanting a salary and going it alone again – submerged me in a confidence crisis.

I made quick tough decisions every day of my life yet when it came to *my* life, I of course struggled.

Dianne is a brilliant florist with an air for the nuance of the families she deals with coupled with a tremendous sense of occasion. She is a strong character and a smart business woman. She gave me that confidence back.

When I confessed to her that London wasn't working for me any more, she urged me to go it alone to which I responded that I couldn't. She was a key supplier to me that she had almost always seemed part of the business. So, the inevitable happened. I would run events, she would run the floristry and we would do both from the magical shit tip of her premises in Deansgate in Manchester. We would spend days chasing her Jack Russell into town!

Roger said it was a mistake.

He didn't mean chasing the dog.

'Do not go into business 50:50,' he urged.

My view was that it was the only ethical stance to take. If I did not make it equal, then I would walk all over her. I was exercising control over my control instincts.

Taylor Lynn Corporation was born.

Every party is different. Every party is the same.

I have never repeated a function. I have retained many elements from what I have done before. There is a difference. Every new gig benefits the following one. Each crazy idea gives you the belief that the next one is also achievable.

The benchmark – The Waldorf.

Working for the same family time and time again tests you. You are rewarded for what you delivered last time by getting the repeat business but of course, you have to re-invent yourself once more. Sibling rivalry can meet parent expectation halfway and that gives you a budget to be creative to exceed the last outing but of course, you can get to the point where you have peaked and might have to peak again. You can imagine the challenge, therefore when a father presents four daughters to you and you know that potentially each party is yours.

So, you can imagine the balancing act between something new and something consistent – it needs the hallmark of me but bears the individual's characteristics.

Good work but hard work.

So the first wanted an elegant dinner at Northcote Manor – a luxury Michellin starred restaurant. The second wanted a brothel theme. The next one walked therough a magic wardrobe to Narnia and the last one wanted a circus theme!

I know.

For Narnia, that meant through the closet of mink coats and into the forest decorated by snow machines and on towards the glass tables with fairy lights.

For the circus, that meant a vintage revolving carousel built into the base of a marquee, a hook a duck game to find where they were sitting and fairground drinks with goldfish in their cocktails. One big thing – 500 little elements. Both were vital.

Then there is the brothel.

My guests arrived in their Bentleys only to be met by two hookers in ocelot coats purring at their entrance. When everyone had gathered, they would begin the party by knocking on the big red door, to be met by an old madam in her 70s with provocative red lipstick on.

Inside, pole dancers in bondage gear. Male dancers on every table.

The result?

Carnage!

Each of these parties had to be both the best and on a par with the previous. In other words, I had to blow them away afresh but leaving them unable to decide who had the better time. That, of course, may simply come down to the individual sister or the dynamic of their crowd. All I could do was leave my own unique mark.

At the heart of such variety and creativity is my constant. Knowing you have a great team of hired staff and suppliers means that at the bullshit end of the deal as the deal takes shape you can say yes with confidence and work out the detail later.

And obviously, every party needs music and around 1997, I solved that problem once and for all.

I met a band.

I wasn't necessarily looking. I was sort of limping from function to function making it up as I went along but as ever a chance encounter ensured permanent status in my life.

I was asked to organise the wedding of a Manchester boy getting married to a French girl. One of her friends played violin in a band. That's how I met and signed the Swan Band.

We have worked together ever since 1997.

They were and remain phenomenal.

I recruited them on the spot – much to the subsequent regret of the father of the groom who to this day wishes that he had come in on the deal.

'Work for me exclusively,' I asked them.

And they said yes.

Remember the context of where I am at here. I am starting afresh but with the knowledge from going solo originally and the London experience. I am in the business of selling an intangible concept and pitching a business proposal that guarantees no work.

Yet, I had the vision and the belief and they had the confidence so we struck a deal and it remains one of the wisest decisions I have ever made.

Nobody has ever said that they are anything other than brilliant. They are the original repeat booking and where I go, they go. In time that means the Manchester Uniteds of this world – from their owners to the club itself.

When I lecture now about party planning, I am fond of saying that nobody ever says the day after an event what a wonderful piece of chicken that was. They say they were pissed and the band was amazing. They are my benchmark.

Once the band is in full swing, to a degree your risk is lessened on the night. These guys will play for five hours and that becomes the centre piece of the party and of course enables you to remedy other logistics that might not be going to plan while the music distracts. The confidence that they bring to a whole event with feet tapping from the off, spills over into every other aspect. They are invaluable for their performance but as part of the framework to the whole night. If catering need five more minutes, then the swan does not flap.

That doesn't mean you stop work when the band strikes up. Far from it, but they are such a slick, talented, professional well-oiled outfit that as long as the mics work and the lighting is good, once they hit that opening number, I can worry a little less and concentrate on something else.

But who are this band and what thought had I given to exporting them around the world?

Everything comes at a price.

Well, first things first, they are French and based there! Secondly, there are fourteen of them.

I do not need to write the next bit obviously but I am sure you can appreciate that in terms of logistics, the paperwork is already stacking up before we get going.

So I am signing a French band which every time I engage for work will then have to fly into the UK and transport on to the venue whilst adding fourteen plus crew and roadies to the headcount. Hotels, food, transport, freight bills…if you want the best party in town then that is what it takes.

Plus they require a fee too!

Over the years they will travel the world with me – from Russia with love to New York New York. What the hell, I am pretty sure they enjoyed their complimentary week at the world famous Sandy Lane Hotel in Barbados too.

Yet, I have been selective in where they work. You don't take everything just to be working and just to be earning. This is a top drawer outfit for a certain type of clientele.

Of course, over time, I have witnessed their act grow from party to party according to the wishes of the hosts and current musical trends. You see them move it along a little each time, tweaking it here and there. After more than two decades, the act is probably a long way from where it started but also add to that the fact that they were a jobbing band with some notoriety in France and now are continually booked out around the world to people with bigger budgets and better values so therefore increased production skill and resource.

It has been a perfect arrangement for both parties.

Perhaps if I hadn't run into them, I might have found another band or may have come across them elsewhere at a later date. All I know is that they are right at the top of my checklist for delivering quality entertainment and I don't have to worry from gig to gig what the entertainment will be like.

Infectious, spontaneous, and consistently a sensation they weave magic through sound and performance. As a performer, you know the worst thing is when you have lost the audience – when you can hear murmuring alongside the vocal or as the lead takes up his narrative in between songs. These guys have crowd control! From the off, the audience are eating out of their hands.

In fact when they have finished *eating* their main course, from nowhere the violin solo begins. If you want to see how to make the gear change from 300 people finishing up their food to hitting the dance floor in seconds then these are the guys to do it.

With that in mind, I would have the dance floor specially made – rip up what was there and start again and then restructure tables and encourage their mounting so you could get up wherever you damn wanted!

Every time you are left with hairs on your neck.

It remains my only successful marriage.

And I like plucking people from nowhere and backing them. Whether it be a designer or a performer, I have always been able to sniff out potential for star quality at a talent's infancy. Simon Cowell, move aside.

I will give people a chance without leaving anything to chance.

I often used a violinist I had spotted on the streets in Manchester. He was simply trying to fund his education. I knew he was better than that.

Busking outside Marks and Spencer in the city centre turned out to be the best thing one Cuban outfit could have done. I just happened to walk past and signed them.

It might seem a risk but I worked according to my gut and they had talent.

I was able to offer them considerable work which they described as 'better than stealing'. That had been their alternative. Unfortunately that relationship *didn't* last. They left in a hurry and without a trace.

Literally, band on the run.

The Swan, however, continues to glide on.

9 The Red Devil Is In The Detail

You probably recall Manchester United captain and legend Roy Keane muttering about prawn sandwiches. You will undoubtedly be aware that by 1992 Sky had changed the face of sports broadcasting forever. Nor will it have escaped you that Manchester United were getting back to their glory years under Sir Alex Ferguson and through the homegrown young so-called *Class of 92.*

In time and at various times, these three elements were all key to the expansion of my creativity, contacts and brand.

A game that had been in the doldrums of crowd trouble, disasters, and expulsion from the European elite found a saviour in satellite television which now broadcasts hundreds of games live per year when there had really only ever been a couple, and top that up with analysis and scrutiny that had never been seen before.

Plus – it was huge for people in the Salford and Manchester area that so much of what Fergie was building was young and local. Manchester United started to win regularly and that meant success needed to be celebrated. Stadia, because of tragedies like Bradford and Hillsborough, were being rebuilt and expanded. TV gave it the showbiz element.

Football was back – but to a level never seen before. And that's where the 'prawn sandwich brigade' had bigger fish to fry.

Corporate hospitality in football was barely getting going but by 1994, Manchester United were on it but without the knowledge, expertise and staff to pave the way. I owe a lot to the Shellmeister.

Michael Edelson had led an interesting life. Once a judge at Miss World, he had earned his nickname from a *Sunday Times* journalist after his reputation for creating numerous cash shell companies. Amongst his credits, legend has it that he faked a Scottish accent to call Aberdeen Football Club in order to speak with Sir Alex Ferguson, whom was then hired. The rest is history.

41

He is also credited with introducing David Beckham to Victoria. The rest is also history!

From 1982, he had been a non-executive director of Manchester United. He introduced me to the club. ! In fact, he not only opened the door me to the football club but also, later on, to Buckingham Palace.

Ferguson, Beckham and Taylor – the three big signings!

And so it begun. One of my longest relationships and arguably the client who would become one of the biggest brands of the world. Today, many of the individuals who straddled that era are clients too. For both parties it was the right thing at the right time and that remains true to this day.

As the game exploded overnight, so did both health and safety and security – areas that would develop into huge industries but at this point were in their infancy.

I didn't really follow the game that closely. In fact, in my naivety, after getting used to organising Cup Finals for Manchester United in the 90s when one year they didn't make it, I began to ask what was going on before it was spelt out to me that 'no Cup Final no party' – indicative of both my lack of knowledge and of how people had just got accustomed to assuming success at Old Trafford.

At the 1999 Cup Final, I somehow managed to pull off the crazy task of splitting ranks. As ever, I would do the Manchester United gig but somehow also agreed to do their opponents' too.

For Newcastle United, losers on the day as part of the sequence that led to Manchester United's treble, that meant a massive ice bar spelling out Newcastle United and – Sting. We made magnificent ice magpies with the clubs scarves round their neck.

We were so used to doing such events for Manchester United that we also got accustomed to not knowing when they would arrive after the match, nor of course, the tone that we should radiate win, lose or draw. Often we would 'tape' the game' and then cut in the footage into a pre-prepared video montage – in essence editing right up to the last minute.

42

They still had the Champions League Final ahead against Bayern Munich but for Newcastle this literally was their Cup Final. If you watched the game, you will know that there was almost nothing to edit into any montage for them! Manchester United won 2-0 on the day.

Yet, the relationship with the club will always be a yardstick to how well I was doing. They were playing in the Champions League. I had to as well.

Players or their representatives started to call the office. They were starting to get to know me and respected my negotiating power. They wanted a party and value for money.

Teddy Sheringham, their England forward and Man of the Match on that afternoon, was to marry the model Nicola Smith. I was called to a couple of meetings with a view to organising their wedding.

On this occasion, I did not get the gig.

But then, as the tabloids were keen to print, nor did Nicola Smith in the end!

Occasionally in my job I get those 'Can't say at this point' type phone calls. My relationship with the club undoubtedly led to the moment everybody still asks me about.

'My daughter is getting married in Ireland very soon,' the voice at the end of the line began.

'Can I take your name please?' I replied, looking for an early indicator as to whom I was dealing with.

'Yes, it is Jackie Adams.'

It didn't register. I never twigged.

'Her fiancé gave me your number…'

There was nothing too unusual or spectacular about this so far.

'You have put on several events where he works.'

That really didn't narrow it down.

Obviously, I asked where that was.

'Manchester United,' she responded.

Of course, Jackie could have just blurted it out at the start but you get there in stages, sussing people out for attitude, and tone. Both of you. It is a game from both sides. A few gentle lobs from her and she can start to work out if I am the real deal.

43

At this point I only just twig.

I make sure there is no over-excitement or lack of composure in my voice. For some reason, I ask her star sign. There was something about her down to earth manner. She is a fellow Pisces like myself. Sometimes, these details are ice-breakers.

Would I be interested in sponsoring the wedding? In other words, that means to do it for next to nothing in exchange for all the publicity you gain for yourself and your suppliers.

I said no.

I felt it was too much of a risk at that stage in my business. I was nervous about a non-profit making event. I am sure most people would have said yes and many have asked me when I saw the ten page or so spread in OK! magazine if I regretted it.

Well – the thrones and the castle in Ireland looked very lavish...but no. No regrets.

If I had done it, it may have opened many doors for me but commercially it was not the right thing to do at that moment in time. I sensed too that by 1999 it was all about their brand and my relationship with the magazine was very young at that stage only to flourish later. As daft as it may sound, I felt that I really would have zero control over the event.

Today, I would approach it differently and have the confidence to do a deal or walk away. Back then, I just declined.

So, that is how I turned down the opportunity of organising the wedding of David and Victoria Beckham.

The relationship with Manchester United has to be the benchmark. Of course, I was doing lots of other work and plenty of other celebrities but if by the dawn of the new millennium I was the party planner to the biggest football club on the planet I must have been doing something right.

Of course, it did not happen overnight and the call from the Beckhams was a yardstick and a reminder of how much the business had grown.

For example, even years earlier I had been working with Sarah Ferguson, the Duchess of York right at the time she was technically exiting the royal family. You probably remember the toe job story with the Texan millionaire John Bryan and how she was perceived as having brought disgrace on the Royal Family.

Two important Fergies, therefore, in my life.

Later I would come to work with her ex-husband Prince Andrew. Royal protocol could understandably be a nightmare. But you could cut through it once you removed the people in the way. I had been told not to discuss his children or his charities but found myself in an eerie atmosphere with butlers pouring drinks in silence. Recent events make me wonder what else was on the 'do not go there' list.

'Sir, I was told not to discuss your children or charities...' I therefore began.

'Let's start with the children, ' he replied.

I have seen this technique many times over the years. It removes the nonsense at their end if you put guests on their guard and limit the areas you can talk about but then you get there all the same and find that they will open up about anything. You become used to it and know how it works but it gives them a safety net under which they can always withdraw but also reminds you who is boss.

Something, of course that I was not used to!

But you can turn down the Royal Family too.

Just prior to the Commonwealth Games in Manchester in 2002, I got a call from the Granada TV mogul Charles Allen sounding me out about my availability. The Queen and one of the biggest sporting events of the year were heading to town. I was in Italy when I took the call and then rang Dianne back home straightaway who stepped in with her inimitable style and delivered. But – a once in a lifetime opportunity passed on!

Back in 1997, it didn't get much bigger than hosting Luciano Pavarotti in Manchester. After the football World Cup of Italia 90, classical music exploded because the song *Nessun Dorma* reverberated around the world. Nearly a decade later, it was still going strong. Everybody wanted a piece of the big Italian singer. Pavarotti, of course, was enormous.

We had him booked in after his concert in Manchester for a gala dinner with hundreds of tables bought. I don't think he really wanted to be there. I resisted the temptation to charge £30 – or three tenors – for entrance but my only recollection of the function is seeing the big guy sitting there eating nothing more than a bowl of spaghetti.

It was a misfit but just like Manchester United, he was one of the biggest stars in the world. I doubt that my portfolio of clients would extend into Italy but it was a measurement of how quickly and successfully we were building this brand that international stars, albeit at the booking of a UK event, were now very much part of my clientele.

That said, I did get to travel too. Work was expanding overseas whether it be a flash UK client who wanted to export the party abroad or if somehow I got introduced to foreign dignitaries.

There was always the element of uncertainty about taking the party to them. It added extra dimensions such as paperwork and freight transfer. Predictably, it didn't always go to plan or go at all.

I had been recommended to the wife of the ruler of Bahrain. I was clueless as to how to pull this off and they weren't much wiser either. I am summoned and the tickets are booked. We arrive. Somebody dies. Function cancelled.

Nothing to do but lounge around in a palatial residence for a week before our return. No drink allowed. Bored out of my brain. Not always as glamorous as you think!

And death was the wildcard that you could never anticipate at any stage in the planning of an event.

In this job, you become embroiled in and occasionally attached to the people who book you. Think about it – you are asked to pull off a spectacular event on a Disney scale for people with far too much money. They want to out do everybody. They want this simply to be the party to remember.

Often these events fall into two categories. Corporate – making a statement to competitors, showing gratitude and style to staff or a family event making a key date in somebody's life.

To truly understand what the client wants, you have to jump the queue of friendship at speed and know them better than those with whom they have spent each day working or living their lives.

That brings one key element. You see their vulnerability and tensions.

You spot that it means so much more to the mother and the father is paying. You recognise the over-bearing and dominating hen-pecked. You try to educate the vulnerable. You can tell who is just going along with it. You become very good at the psychology very quickly.

Which two elements can throw you the wildcards beyond the non-arrival of suppliers and equipment? People and the weather.

Over the years, I have planned well and backed myself that I could even function in a hurricane. I can spot the time-wasters, bad payers and those who are likely to ring up on the Monday after and complain about something so unnecessary.

Clearly, I have stringent measures in place to legislate for both and I have been here a million times. I know that most people who might have a whinge after will always do so about the tiniest of things. The big picture stuff they rarely mention. My safeguard of course is that most of their guests can't remember other than what a brilliant party it was!

47

If you ask somebody on the day they go back to work and talk about how the party was many will refer to the showpiece at the centre of it – or the band and can't recall much more. They come for the unforgettable.

The ultimate curveball is death.

When you have been doing this as long as I have now, you will have seen most things.

Nobody expected that news when we woke at 7 am on Sunday 31 August 1997.

On the Friday, I had almost done the unthinkable and pulled a card which is always more of a threat than one to deal as an Ace.

I am building a marquee in Cheshire. We are about to host 300 people on the Sunday.

The two elements I describe above – the nit-picker and reluctant payer meet death head on.

I have only once pulled an event.

This is not me being arsey. It is basic economics. You can't put on a party if you have to worry about paying people – and I have to pay a lot of people too who will, notwithstanding regular work from me, have cleared their diaries and put my event to the top of their list.

If I am providing for 300 people then I am paying the wages of at least 60 people plus sourcing and designing everything from material to menus. And I have to pay whether or not the event goes ahead.

I have never had an overdraft and always settle up within seven days. I know that if you live beyond your means then you spend your life on egg shells. That has been so much of my motivation to avoid that.

In short, do not leave it until 48 hours before the event to pay me. Or you will be left explaining to 300 people where the event has gone!

That would rarely get to that point of course because the type of clientele that I entertain would lose so much in reputation if their big do did not happen and the reason was simply that they hadn't paid. Embarrassment can be hugely motivating!

48

You can tell early on if the client has respect for you and if they can afford it. These were quite lacking of respect and understanding of what we were trying to create.

I had had enough.

The money had been coming all week. It is not that difficult to pay somebody. The money *hadn't* been coming all week.

I pulled the florists. I told the lighting guys to pack up and go home. Then, with their house a bombsite with half unpacked boxes and crew equipment everywhere and their own possessions having being stored away, I marched into to see the host and broke the news to him:

'It's off,' I told him.

'Nobody is doing anything until the money is in.'

I turned around and left.

I sound like a diva. *It* sounds dramatic. But you have to be as ballsy in saying 'no'.

Think it through. What alternatives do you have? You, yourself can't get that tag of someone who didn't get paid. Work out that damage in future negotiations with both potential clients and suppliers. You have to take a stand.

Miraculously, he was able to rustle up a same day transfer.

You had to do what you had to do. Generally, I react well to stress like this. If you control the situation then you can determine the outcome.

However, back on and when I arrive at work at 7 am on the Sunday that was a situation none of us had any power over.

Princess Diana has been killed in a car crash in the early hours in a tunnel in Paris.

The whole country stops.

Details are inevitably sketchy at first and on a Sunday, people probably wake up at the greatest cross-section of times than any other day. Some people still did not know by lunchtime; others had seen the story move on at a pace from the early hours. Prince Charles was already in the air, bound for the French capital.

49

One by one sporting events got pulled. Mainstream television just shut down everything. Motorways and traffic in general were noticeably slower. There were only a few mobiles and no social media so Heaven only knows how we coped back then (!) but word spread and everyone was gripped.

For somebody that few people knew but millions felt they did, it represented a huge outpouring of grief never really seen in my lifetime. I don't know why this was the case but whilst Diana could manipulate the press as well as anyone, you always felt that there was something landmark and courageous in her that changed the game.

Divorcee, mum of two, land mine warrior, possibly about to marry a Muslim, the nation didn't seem to fall out of love with her when she became persona non grata to the Royal Family. In fact, here was the underdog in all her Versace style, forever in their faces and changing the establishment beyond the point of return. Tony Blair, the then Prime Minister, using all his persuasive oratory skills dubbed her The People's Princess. And it stuck.

On the same day that we lost our princess I still had to put on a show for 300 people.

Of course there were many people on that day who had events planned and went ahead but most could not help but feel distracted. It didn't matter if you were a monarchist or not, everybody was rocked by the news *and* the manner of the tragedy.

Moments like this can throw into doubt events like mine and people's recollection of them afterwards which is key to my business. The anecdotal sell, when people said that they had a great time and I am '*the* person to book' is what keeps getting me hired.

Given the fuss over getting paid, there was no way I was pulling this event twice nor was I holding out much hope for positive feedback. In the end, a huge cost has been paid out and 300 guests are 300 guests who all turn out even though the nation has stopped. I, too, have my staff who will be affected by various level of grief and shock according to their own personal views and emotions in life.

For eighteen hours we are in a bubble.

We throw the best party you can for these people at this price and that is the party we were always planning. We do not walk around in a trance nor do we under-perform because of the day and its challenges.

We get the job done. With satisfaction and professionalism. We close ourselves off to the outside world and deliver.

The next day we return to the reality and a very sombre Britain.

Through circumstance and clientele, this rates as my most numbing party and a day of which I recall little else.

For Diana, it was the end. For us, the show must go on.

One of the realities of working for a club and a business like Manchester United is that you instantly realise that those two elements are locked together. That is to say that the *club* drives the *business* but also the *business* drives the *club*.

Having been in 'before the beginning' of 'corporate football' which essentially is the Sky era post 1992, I think I can measure this as well as anyone.

Now, when you are working with this business so regularly, you learn one thing. What happens on the pitch and the circus around the cast who perform on it is unpredictable. You can never know if a Roy Keane is going to get arrested, if a David Beckham is going to get married, if the team will score two goals in – frankly – *beyond* the final minutes of a Champions League Final.

You are dealing with massive stars and the consequence of their performances on and off the pitch. You prepare, as a businesswomen, and party planner as you do any event but this is the field where external events – other than the weather – can play the biggest part in throwing a curveball.

It could be something as simple as a delayed kick-off or extra time on match day or it could be something that has nothing to do with the match but has consumed the club or the sporting world.

Two examples stand tool.

By 2002, the English football manager was the Swede Sven-Goran Eriksson. Even though this was new territory in that it was the first time the national side had employed a foreign coach, I recall the nation warming to him.

He had a reputation in football – I am told – for pulling off results when it mattered and none resonated more than England beating Germany 5-1 in Munich with a Michael Owen hat trick.

That ticked a lot of boxes early in his reign and meant that the heat was off him. He had done something nobody else had done – walloped Germany in their own back yard and the other darling of English football after David Beckham had cemented that wonderkid image he forged on the back of that goal at the France World Cup in 1998 during the match Beckham was sent off in.

Despite being foreign, he came across as English but with all those bits you want to take from Sweden such as charm, sex appeal and a masterful command of English language that added to his suave nature.

I fancied the pants off him.

Unfortunately so did the TV personality Ulrika Jonsson and she managed to get them. Outside of Abba and the IKEA brand, the two most famous Swedes in the UK were at it.

The 'scandal' of two unmarried individuals hit the press. It would disrupt England's chances at the football World Cup, now just a couple of months away. Sven, of course, had been living with the Italian lawyer Nancy Dell'Olio in London but hey essentially they were sort of free to go!

To their 'credit' Sven just got up and got on with his job the day the story broke, attending the Chelsea versus Manchester United match. So did Ulrika sat about 100 yards away with her friend the TV presenter Angus Deayton, who himself was also turned over by the British tabloids later that year.

I can't say if this was the Swedish way just to crack on or if they had an open attitude to fidelity. I do know two things – that if he had left it a week or so and laid low then the press would have hounded him and it would have been even more of a drama when he finally re-emerged at a football match (and this was a guy who would often go to two games in a day so he was very visible). The other note I make was that Sven, on the biggest salary anyone in that role had ever had, previously was reported to have complained that the worst thing about working in the country was the press.

Now, he was the story.

So, timing is everything.

What is next on my schedule?

Ah, a breakfast for the Manchester United Foundation – hosted by Angus Deayton, and featuring Sven and Ulrika.

53

The Sven story is not actually a Manchester United story, though an uneasiness began between him and the nation at this point which somewhere along the line did lead to the speculation that he might replace Sir Alex Ferguson on his retirement. For now, he was booked as a speaker as he would often be around the country. I do not recall why Ulrika was also hired for this event. Angus, as you may know, is a big red and a very witty host.

So – this is where the club and the business collide.

400 keen sports fans have paid good money for a good cause to see good guests. Now, realistically there was a chance that none of them might show.

To many people's surprise – all three turned up.

The room was buzzing. I have never felt that murmur in the hubbub prior to any event. Everybody had so much they wanted to ask and know yet clearly these people are not hungry journalists so become a little tongue-tied.

When they booked the tickets they thought they would get a Champagne breakfast and get their photo taken with the England boss whilst the funny guy off the TV cracks a few jokes. Now they found themselves in a room with two of the people at the heart of the biggest showbiz story of the year.

That was the randomness of the job. This was the example of the wildcard in event planning.

Obviously, I couldn't have been happier once I saw they were all there. It turned a charity breakfast into a money can't buy ticket.

But they did.

So for all the times I had learnt that the show must go on. Here were other people looking down the barrel of media scrutiny who also followed suit.

And Sven was sexy – magnetic with naughty eyes and had a way with women. A charismatic boy who looked you straight into the bones.

I admired his balls.

Though obviously not as Ulrika had.

Performances on the pitch meant that the *business* of Manchester United had high value for myself and for the club.

Around Manchester, it had incredible worth. If I needed anything and said that it was the club, doors opened every time and at speed. Manchester City, at this point, were not really in the game. They didn't even move to their new stadium until 2003.

For the football, the key moment ahead would be (after a couple of false starts) the season after Sir Alex Ferguson retired. That end finally came in 2013.

Before that the other pivotal moment had arrived. And everybody was watching. Not long into the new millennium the Glazer family from the United States had begun acquiring a stake in the football club finally taking control by May 2005.

These guys were big fish with a track record running the Tampa Bay Buccaneers back home. Some protests continue to this day – many United fans were concerned about the deal and the re-shaping of debt it seemed to attract.

For everybody really it was an uncertain time. To the football viewer outside of the city, you would still look and see the results at the weekend. To everyone connected with the club, who knew how the Americans would run a British institution?

What would I have done in that scenario? Probably, the same as most people who are successful in business – identified the key individuals who made the club tick...then bring in my own people. I would run an entire personnel check from top to bottom and look at everything from the cleaner to the catering, from IT to seeing who really was *it* on the pitch.

Many business who enter new administrations deliberately rip up everything to make a statement. Others have to as they have acquired something either in crisis or not yet fulfilling its potential.

With the track record of running an NFL franchise and all their other business interests, you really could not be so complacent as to think that a few thousand miles would keep you safe. These were businessmen on a global scale from a country where sport, entertainment, and hospitality were on a different level.

It was time to get smart.

The first thing that struck me straightaway was their security. *That* made a statement. But there was a lot of hostility towards them and they were very wealthy people.

To get close to them was near impossible.

I knew I just had to carry on delivering for the club and that at some point they would ask who that lady was...

Thankfully, it didn't take long.

One of the sons Bryan was at a function where my band stole the show once again.

'Who are that band?' he asked.

That was all I needed.

My French musicians delivered once more and I would continue to do so for the club for a long period of time ahead.

I was in.

I was *in* anyway.

Now, I was in from a position of strength.

Sometimes when you are organising a party somebody will nervously joke 'What could possibly go wrong?' The answer of course is everything. Over the years, journalists and students like to know what did.

The golden rule is this. You do not go into an event having left anything to chance. You are a well-polished machine and your suppliers and staff get the drill. They have been here countless times with you. They get it.

So, beyond taking out very complicated insurance, that grey area of 'I didn't see that coming' is an entirely special section all by itself.

If you are a professional in this game, only two things can derail you – stupidity or the unexpected.

Both smacked each other in the face on Remembrance Sunday 2004.

Destination: The Midland Hotel. Time: 4 pm on the Sunday. Event: A Jewish wedding.

My bread and butter perhaps. I have been here so many times before – both the venue and the job type.

Dates are dates in the calendar and most weekends are busy. Some obvious events need avoiding like Manchester hosting the Commonwealth Games.

Ashamedly, I had no foresight to think that Sunday 14 November would present any kind of issue. You can probably appreciate that the wedding was in the diary for a considerable period of time and whilst Remembrance Sunday also could make that claim, it did slightly move around the calendar, dependant on where in the week the 11th fell.

Plus when you accept the booking months in advance, you have no chance of getting advance information so long into the future as to what might be happening where and when.

So, we cracked on – the band flew over from Paris. I booked out the Premier Inn in Manchester for them. Just another busy weekend of organising, creating and delivering. Party time.

Not quite. Problem.

Our van was towed away.

Now, potentially, no band and no party.

The clock was ticking fast all the way until 4 pm.

Of all the situations to talk myself out of, how on earth could you explain this one to the family? Excuses work from the end of the problem. You can quite easily understand somebody getting irate and asking 'well surely you knew it was Remembrance Sunday?'

Obviously you did but it is not something you factor in until the signs start going up a week or so before and even then, Manchester has a wealth of roads in and access points that you just assume you will be OK. I have worked around ten kilometre road races and Manchester United parades and never had a problem.

Never assume. Note going forward – always check date clashes, however random the date may appear to you.

The race against time is on. I have fourteen musicians with no kit and no clothes. That is not going to make a good night.

I try to bribe security at the pound where the vehicle is being held. He is not interested.

'More than my job is worth, love,' he stonewalls me in that stereotypical tone of the man on the gate.

This, after all, is what he is there for. Everybody turns up with a sob story of how it wasn't their fault and how they have been hard done by. It probably was worth more than his job was worth but it was my actual job and hey, if he had shown some leniency I would have hired him myself.

What to do next?

I have no options.

I go to the police station – at top speed.

I am getting nowhere. In short, there is no way anyone can be contacted to make that decision and if there were that truck would not be going anywhere until well after the parades.

Twenty minutes later I burst into tears.

You have to do what you have to do.

I was somewhere between acting that out and genuinely feeling it. No scenario to this point had tested me this much. You wonder if you have given them too much information. Perhaps if I had told them that I needed it by midday, they might have let me have it at one. They knew I had to be in position by 4 – though even that was way past the last chance saloon.

If you have ever sat in a police station, you will know that it is the waiting that kills you. An empty building and a skeleton staff on a Sunday morning…a couple of drunks and some minor detentions. Everybody has that feeling of 'why can't they just deal with me now…what is the wait about?' Something about such a set of circumstances makes everyone wonder why they are not at the front of the queue.

I can't give a cop a backhander.

Obviously.

But I would be prepared to pay almost anything to get my stuff released.

In the end they take £750.

I have no idea where that figure came from and I am not particularly bothered. I don't have time to argue.

I tear to the synagogue at Whitefield, Manchester. The mother of bride is just about to walk down the aisle. My team are managing the procession.

'Is everything OK?' She asks.

'Of course,' I reply.

From here, I have to present a front and radiate confidence knowing that it *will* be alright on the night. The truck is en route!

Nobody ever sees what goes on behind the scenes – no one need ever know. One element of the event always presents a smokescreen for another. With all eyes on the service, nobody was even thinking about the truck. Whilst that was my now, it was their later.

Remembrance Sunday – lest we forget.

I would do well to remember.

13 Runaway Train

By 2005, the TV show *Coronation Street* was right alongside Manchester United Football Club as both a regular and an A List client. I was not daft. I knew that it sent out a message that if you were trusted to work with both, others would follow.

It was basic economics – both were major brands and successful. They were Manchester icons and sold around the world. Each of them did massive amounts for charity, often looking at magazine deals for that aspect or for its cast and players. Their shows and teams made stars and at any given moment, someone else would walk into their slipstream – just like Eamonn Holmes being a regular at matches.

It ticked every box and creatively was right up there.

So, over the years my relationship blossomed and Manchester can be a bit like that. When you start, you look in on a closed shop, but if you do the work and hang around long enough, suddenly you are through the door and part of the furniture.

So, I had done the hard yards simply by seeking out the set builders from the Granada studio tours right at the start of the career. I didn't for one moment think that would take me where it has. I just needed that gig to come off and in the process spotted the opportunity that the tours presented! Corrie was based there. From then on, I began to do little bits for Jane Mclure at the Tours. It was she who later introduced me to Charles Allen. That is how the process starts.

Never throw away a contact nor under-estimate the power of who you meet and getting to know them early when you are starting off.

Fast forward a few years and Jenny McAlpine is in touch. Jenny is famous for playing Fizz Brown in the soap since 1997 but of course, there is so much more to her than meets the eye.

Since the age of seventeen, she has been helping deprived children in Egypt through the Thebes Project and her own father, the late Thomas McAlpine OBE set the tone for the parts of her life you don't always see. Thomas passed away in 2017 but spent over 40 years working in mental health and healthcare. That influence stays with Jenny to this day.

Her father formed the charity Moodswings in 1999.

I recognised early the worth on so many levels of working with charities. Sometimes, there is a perception that because it is for a good cause then your services are for free. That is a little daft – you still have to provide catering, venues bands etc and pay staff to work on the night. Equally many charities do make money. For you, there was often great kudos in being involved and it opened countless doors to people and organisations that had their charity at heart without really knowing how to put on a show and whose public figures (such as their patrons) might often be inaccessible. Almost universally, their dedication to the cause was total. That didn't mean that they were entertainers. So, it is a juggling act but very early on, I worked this out and realised that I needed to set a new tariff at a reduced rate if I was to work with charities. Equally, you can't do them all or you wouldn't have a business. Nor would you appear sincere if you were working with every charity.

I agreed to work with Jenny and Moodswings on a casual understanding that over time I might be able to acquire some work from Corrie. She didn't have the authority to act on behalf of the show obviously but there were always milestones associated with it and a cast that ranged from the newish younger members of her era to the older mainstays like William Roache who had played Ken Barlow since Episode One – and that was in December 1960!

I sensed that if I built the trust, this could be very good for everyone and so it was with long-lasting work relationships and friendships about to form.

Antony Cotton, who has played Sean Tully since 2003, was about to celebrate his 30th birthday. Like Jenny, he was from the Bury area. Together we earmarked one of the focal points of East Lancashire tourism to celebrate his landmark birthday.

The only thing was – this was new territory.

I was used to working with big names and events but now I have to take charge of around hundred celebs, all of whom you see on the TV every day whether in the show or at awards ceremonies. These are household names – big stars in the UK without being (mostly) starry. One celeb event often means countless celebs at their event.

Oh, and he wants the party on a train!

The East Lancs Railway is an old style line which runs through Ramsbottom, Rawtenstall and terminates at Bury. Over the year it hosts many themed nights and excursions from Santa trains to *Thomas the Tank Engine* to Murder Mystery Nights.

But it had never taken on anything like this.

The problems stack up from the off. The first issue is that essentially you are dealing with old, dusty carriages that if you clean like a domestic goddess still retain that old look. That, is of course, part of its charm in a country where railways are often derided for not being what they used to be.

Then of course you have to legislate for carriages. How on earth do you put on a function with food and live music when a single section of the train holds only a few people and there are interlocking joining sections between?

Add to that fancy costumes – stars like to dress and someone always gets splattered with litter or leaves at a train station. Nor did I want people hanging around on a platform, literally waiting for a train. Then, once they board, we have to serve drinks and music while the train meanders its way to its destination. Stretch that journey out because it is not a long one. Literally, a moveable feast of problems.

I start with a Champagne reception, dreading someone having too many too soon and losing their footing and a heel at the platform's edge. I overload the station with flowers and old style luggage to create a nostalgia look. It is an old-school train after all. I create a party space on the platform and on the train and then I pull my master stroke.

I have disguised several entertainers to mingle in. So when Antony thinks the train driver is making his way down the platform that is in fact an actor. Likewise, the ticket collector has never inspected before in his life. Oh, and the waiters, they are all singers ready to perform at every stage of the journey.

I love this party because it represents a blueprint of what we do.

Antony is a very smart guy and very clear in what he wants and what works. So, I sit down with him to work on the night and I have to answer the standard which is 'So what exactly am I getting for my money?' and I offer my usual 'trust me' and these are words that translate into no roadmap for the event! Remember too that Antony and his friends are actors and are used to lines, props, positions and event management. He rightly wants to know what his party will be yet his party will be nothing if I don't hold back the singing waiters and the station manager! Trust is everything and you have to walk that line between letting a star stage manage an event and telling them nothing. If you take away that ability to radiate surprise onto your guests, you are probably not going to succeed.

Plus, there was the security aspect too. By and large, the Manchester mafia left the Corrie stars to be. Occasionally there would be some negative story if one of the cast had run into a bit of bother in their personal lives but generally the press left this close-knit community to get on with their lives.

This was different – and too good an opportunity.

I guess it is almost impossible to invite a ton of celebs and their partners to an open air event on a landmark tourist attraction and send that party on the pre-determined route that the East Lancs Railway takes without someone blabbing. Generally, the cast knew discretion was key because they lived potentially under that glare all their life. All it takes though is someone – perhaps a partner who doesn't have to live so cautiously – to book in for a hair appointment and when asked what the occasion is to give the game away in the interests of making small talk.

This is a massive part of the job. Never mind the challenge of serving food and drink through the carriages which I principally overcame by devising a traditional Lancashire hotpot. At every stop on the journey, I had to get my team out first and clear the bushes from the little tittering of excitement that would greet us.

I had a magazine deal riding on this as ever. I couldn't have paparazzi swinging from the trees like Tarzan.

I like the challenge of working with Antony. He *challenged* me. It is that fine line. I need total control of that event and always try to avoid the meddling mother of the bride scenario but through Lorraine and Dianne, I had always worked best sparking off creative people who had a vision too. I think I need people like that in my life who will take me on but then know how to back down at the end and give me the last word!

On that basis of spark and vision, our friendship was formed.

Potentially ahead, he would have other landmark birthdays. Life tended to work like that after all! There would be other Corrie dos. They all saw my work and word was spreading that this was another Liz Taylor job.

Before long stars like Catherine Tyldesley (Eva), Suranne Jones (Karen Mcdonald) and Katherine Kelly (Becky McDonald) would also enter my world.

Parties, magazines, anniversaries, leaving-dos but most importantly friendships at the heart of Britain's favourite TV show meant business was good and life was much better.

And then I am asked to do the Corrie 50th party. This is a massive deal. The soap will also air a live episode.

At 2 am on the morning of the biggest party the show has ever seen, I get a call from the police. The alarm is going off at the lock-up where my red roses are stored. Are all my flowers stolen? They are loaded in three vans in the warehouse. It is always the bloody flowers. Millions of them set to go to the town hall. Gone.

I tear into town, racing against time.

You guessed it.

I am done for speeding.

I decide to chance my arm and write to the police to explain.

There is no real explanation, is there? You can't really talk yourself out of this one, can you?

I am stunned to receive the reply a couple of weeks later.

'My wife is a huge Corrie fan,' it read. 'On this occasion, I will let you off.'

More than one reason to open the fizz.

14 The Stars Are coming Out Tonight

To be asked to organise Corrie's 50th birthday party was a dream come true. When Charles Allen was at the helm, I had also taken on their 40th…but this was the big one. Obviously, it is an excellent piece of business but if you remove yourself from that, wow. Here I am as the legendary TV show – the only mainstay of our schedules bar the news since pretty much day one and something I grew up watching – celebrates a landmark anniversary.

It means a lot to someone who grew up within a stone's throw of it and has seen thousands of episodes. Now, I can also count the show's creator Tony Warren as a friend.

By 2010, the figures speak for themselves – over 100 deaths, nearly a ton of marriages and dozens of barmaids. We had lived with the ever-evolving drama and some of it had stayed the same.

All eyes were watching for the 50th. The show itself would also air a live episode. Granada and I chose The Hilton for a star-studded charity event.

Whilst revelling in its own glory, the show never lost its heart at the centre of the community nor that feeling that it had a social responsibility to give something back.

A private event in a golden and black theme, the evening was as much an acknowledgement of its achievement as anything else, crawling back through hours of archive to unearth priceless footage, much of which today's cast probably had never previously seen such as the great Hilda Ogden singing in the bath to Stan and countless shots of the legendary Annie Walker. The show never forgot its roots.

They needed the party too – and even though there was huge press interest in the celebrations, most people were looking the other way. The show had aired every night for a week under the billing Four Funerals and a Wedding following an explosion at a local bar, which – no surprise was not the Rovers! – and as a result a tram crashed from the viaduct into The Kabin and the

Corner Shop. What followed was carnage. Only soaps look to mark their key anniversaries with such death and destruction.

Fourteen million people watch the deaths of long-serving cast members Ashley Peacock (Steven Arnold) and Molly Dobbs (Vicky Binns), an emergency marriage between Peter Barlow (Chris Gascoyne) and Leanne Battersby (Jane Danson), a confession to Sally Webster (Sally Dynevor) that her husband Kevin (Michael Le Vell) had recently fathered Molly's baby and the live TV birth of Fizz's (Jenny McAlpine) premature baby Hope – believed to be the first live acting out of a birth on TV alongside the first computer-generated imagery on a live show.

It was the programme's record TV audience for seven years. A cast of sixty plus actors and a crew of over 300 worked their magic.

The press interest was colossal.

Even to the degree that, in the absence of any leaks, *The Sun* chose to fabricate an article that there had been an Al-Qaeda terror threat for during the live show. Greater Manchester Police confirmed that there had been no such warning. It was an unnecessary and disrespectful distraction on a day when there was so much goodwill to the show.

What remains extraordinary is that despite all this inconvenience – the police cordoning off the crime scene, gas and fire everywhere, several deaths and a newborn on the way, all of them managed to rise from the debris to party!

You wouldn't know Jennie had been through such a trauma just a few hours before.

But they then had always got the tone right – their close knit group delivering high quality on screen and largely behaving with discretion and humility off it.

Three years later, it was the end of the road for the old Granada Studios set too. Much of the media, from the BBC to production companies, were moving to the brand new Media City at Salford Quays. This really was the end of the era. TV sets come and go but so many people had played out such great storylines on those cobbles, it was hard to think that it would be no more.

Of course, Media City was built for a brand new era which would serve them well and in line with changes in technology but Corrie wanted one last hurrah on the old street.

So, I built a marquee and the fascias of the houses became the walls of that structure and we saw out the old venue in style.

This three year period from just before the 50th to the farewell probably cemented my relationship with the individuals on the show as much as with the show itself.

Individuals like Jenny were coming to me.

I was asked to organise the wedding of Lucy-Jo Hudson and Alan Halsall in 2009. As Katy Harris and Tyrone Dobbs they had *both* been in the show. But these *are* normal people – they are still bride and groom – but you do expect a little something extra from a real life Corrie wedding.

Often the desire to do that magazine deal and stand out from the crowd can produce that odd quirky request.

For Lucy-Jo and Alan, they went for a Ritz style with a white baby grand piano in the middle of the room. Not after Alan, always up for a fun, had arrived at the church dressed as…Batman, and in a car to match.

OK! certainly got value for their money.

Catherine Tyldesley, who had played Eva Price and then went on to star in *Strictly*, asked me to organise her baby shower. I became good friends with Kym Marsh (Michelle Connor) who did a lot of charity work. She had suffered her own losses in real life.

Sally Lindsay had long since left her role as Shelley Unwin when she asked me to arrange her wedding to her partner of ten years – the drummer Steve White. The marriage was to be held just before Christmas and consequently they wanted the full on festive theme in a pub overlooking a seasonal setting and with traditional Christmas meal – a ceremonial white Christmas into a gold and green feast for dinner.

Here was a great example of a normal, lovely couple having their special day but slipping back into the role for a few hours because of the magazine deal. For the Corrie stars, their agents will talk to *Hello!* And *OK!* Certain criteria need to be met and that often involves liaising with the other cast members, which most are happy to do as they may well ask the same favour in the future.

Logistically, it can be a nightmare for both magazine and the couple. It might involve hanging around for three or four hours and will require a variety of shots from family to cast but there won't be a deal without all the key personnel. The magazines know that if I am at the business end of the agreement on the day then it is likely to get done a lot more efficiently. I take the pressure away from the couple, sort security and avoid the long range lens and deliver the goods in around 40 minutes.

For Sally and Steve, that meant friends and family but also Alan Carr, Gok Wan, Suranne Jones and Carol Vorderman.

Amidst all this choreography, the spontaneous moments are the best – Andy Whyment who plays Kirk Sutherland got up to sing with the band from The Commitments at Sam Aston's recent wedding in a Cheshire barn.

The stars like to come out of character too and put their own marker on their day. Simon Gregson (Steve McDonald) swerved his opening dance on his big day by launching into a hilarious and ridiculous beatbox interpretation of their special song.

It is easy to forget these are normal people. I make sure every wedding has a personal touch – mine. I know that someone else will book me because of what they see on the day. There can't be a much greater endorsement than the nation's longest running TV show.

15 A Little Extra Corrie

Sometimes I am a fan too. I am always a fan. I have to pinch myself that I get to work with people who work on the TV show I grew up watching. I have never tired of watching *Coronation Street*. My perspective obviously changed as I was asked to organise their charity functions, their anniversary parties and then individuals' personal events but I remain a fan – always have been, always will.

Growing up in a completely different era of Britain, Corrie stood for the North for the working class, for industrial roots, for that gritty humour and of course, for high quality drama.

There has been nothing like it and it has aired for so long now there never will be. What is the closest thing to it that there has ever been on telly? Perhaps *Crossroads*? After two incarnations, that has come and gone. *EastEnders*, while huge in its day, just doesn't have the same warmth as the show that evolved on our doorstep.

That may be the key. It was always real and even when it has suspended disbelief with occasional moments of madness like the tram crash its character has been at its heart and that is – at the risk of writing like a cliché – at the heart of northern life.

I have sat through so many episodes where nothing happened – ordering a pint in The Rovers with two lines of dialogue must be the most repeated scene in the history of television but somehow the glow and the wit always shine, proving you don't need big drama, big stars and big effects to make it work.

They have of course had all three over the years but I think the measurement is how often you see a character just bed in in the background and then you look up ten years later and you don't even realise that they haven't only just appeared on screen.

Of course, for my era Jack and Vera were icons – did this bickering couple ever have great storylines or did they just argue?! My signed photo of the actress Liz Dawn adorns my wall. Hilda Ogden, played by Jean Alexander, was unexceptional in her character definition but the way she defined that role was incredible. The nagging northern housewife with cutting put downs became a star. Elsie Tanner, played by Pat Phoenix – well, that is me, folks!

Over the years, some of the cast have fled the nest – Michelle Keegan went to star in projects such as the military drama *My Girl*. Katherine Kelly (Becky McDonald) starred in *Miss Selfridge*. Sarah Lancashire, who played dippy Raquel, has dominated so many BBC1 and ITV dramas. Denise Welch became a panellist on *Loose Women* and so on and so on, but the mainstays stayed and stayed forever. That is also at the core of its success. Ken Barlow, for example, played by William Roache, is unlikely to ever get a massive storyline again but he is part of the furniture there and might only get to buy a newspaper these days but there is always a nod and wink to the legendary storylines of the past and his love triangle with Deidre and Mike Baldwin even though it was more than three decades ago. The writing is so skilful that the heritage of the show is never forgotten despite new faces and returning old ones. The show is the star and the stars know it. They live and breathe it.

As a viewer it does make you proud of your Northern roots. From an early age it was all I knew. It felt like northern life. It seemed real and the experience of watching it seemed collective.

Not only did I get to know the cast extremely well over the years but I became friends with the people who made the cast great – Tony Warren, the show's creator amongst them. Plus, if it hadn't been for that chance conversation right at the start of all this then I may not have run into the crew at the Granada Studios tour which proved to be a pivotal moment in the foundation of the business.

From time to time, you have to call in a favour – for yourself. It was time to get the bucket list out.

'Do you not think I should be on the show?' I asked Simon Gregson at his wedding.

Simon had been in the show since 1989 – he was just fifteen when he made his first appearance. Playing Steve McDonald has been his life.

The fact of the matter is that I get my hair done twice a week and hair and beauty is part of me, so I was desperate to be a customer in Audrey's salon. The reality is that when you are on set, it can be quite soul-destroying. Shop fronts were just that and no more, and if you ran up to the stop of a flight of stairs, you got the brick wall of a TV set at the top. The process of making drama is quite grim and...undramatic.

And boy, did I land the plum part. Oh yes, I can hear my name being called at the National Television Awards. This is it. My role in the nation's number one soap was sure to be recognised.

Er, no.

I turned up all made up with my Chanel bag wanting to shine. I had had my hair freshly done. They took my bag off me and told me not to open my mouth and as you might expect, I am hanging around for hours, waiting to sit in Roy's Rolls – the café owned by Roy Cropper. My Oscar performance consists of nodding, facing a wall with my back to the door.

I didn't quite need an agent at this point.

I had no character name and I had no lines. I wore my own clothes. But I was on and in and felt part of it. It was a dream come true for all its banality!

In fact, it was so much fun doing nothing that I wanted to do it again. So, I did.

Sally Lindsay had become a good friend. Like many, including Simon Gregson, she did her time serving behind the bar at The Rovers Return. On any given scene there must have always been extras milling about.

Could I play the part of a posh bird sitting in the background sipping half a coke? Yes, I will just turn up as myself and for this one special occasion...water down the drink from something stronger.

It takes your relationship with the show you already loved to a new level. Long days, hanging around, high pressure to deliver that quality of writing, production and acting several times per week leaves you in awe.

It is something that I can always say that I have done now – twice but of course, every time I watch my admiration increases – as does my amusement.

Knowing that Simon or Antony or whoever is playing a blinder in character and yet knowing them personally too whilst watching your favourite TV show, well aware of where the edits are and the fact that it is not really beer in that glass or that door didn't lead anywhere on set is a complicated business.

That I still get sucked in is a credit to the show.

I am not sure why they haven't asked me back since though!

Antony's party was new territory. Party on the move.

But then things got a little crazy.

'I want to do something nuts,' a client announced to me.

His daughter's 18th was imminent.

So, I hired a rooftop of a hotel on Great John Street in Manchester and transformed the area into a nightclub with all my waitresses wearing massive Perspex trays attached to their hips! It is funny how people come round to your crazy opening thoughts as they watch your mad idea slowly become acceptable and reality. They have to take it on trust.

There was more...

If you don't ask, you don't get.

For the 18th, I had a huge cake made with insane detail. It was a replica of the young lady's bedroom with hair dryers and handbags and books by the bedside table – all edible and part of the display.

You can buy rich people anything – and they can shell out huge amounts of cash in the process but there is no substitute for the eye of the creative that can produce *money can't buy* presentation like this. They were delighted.

It took four guys to shift.

But that wasn't even the moment.

'What would you like...?' I began...

'More than anything...in a theoretical world...if I said nothing was any problem...and I would make it happen.'

This is a jokey conversation that you do have with the wealthy clients from time to time. I had had it frequently. There are also no boundaries. For the super rich. Some things you can pull off, others you just can't get near. One thing I do know is that someone answers this question with the craziest Bucket List item, there is equal chance you can persuade someone to do it for nothing as much as pay them a million.

It is all about charming your way in and getting the little black book *out*.

'What would you like?' I asked my mega client second time.

I had no inkling what his answer would be.

I loved asking the question for that reason. It gave you insight into the real them, what might be the actual size of their budget and that, of course, was good for me.

Anyone laying down a challenge my way with the almost unspoken caveat that they know something is out of the question only drives me on to move the goalposts even further.

If you say it can't be done, then that becomes my focus and of course builds the myth and legend of my brand from which word gets around. In today's world that is so different. It is one thing in the 1980s to build an enchanted castle and word spread amongst the bar mitzvah audience that this is the new – well, *bar*. Today, in the social media world where every business in the world self-promotes, the legend takes no time at all to gain momentum and stays in the public domain forever.

That is great for me and for the business. It also provokes the next conversation when a subsequent client arrives and says 'so you can re-create *Wicked* and get Diana Ross, yeah?'...the game is upped and one rich person wants to out-do the next...the challenge of ego-driven wealth spills over into my company.

As ever, I always say yes and deal with the consequences after.

My client was weighing up whether or not he was about to say something stupid. It didn't matter if he could afford it.

Could I get it?

Was he about to embarrass himself by literally asking for the impossible or might he show that his money had placed him out of touch of what really was achievable?

The answers always come tentatively.

Nobody rich likes to be laughed at.

'I would like Harry Styles to bring the cake out for my daughter,' he asked.

'No problem,' I replied.

I called in a favour through a contact of my elder daughter. A young man with a bigger black book than mine!

The common ground of charity brought so many people together under the umbrella of 'good cause'. It was only afterwards that many people realised that they were in effect also the biggest networking events.

It was time to call the man in the know back.

'I need to borrow Harry Styles,' I told him.

'No problem,' he also replied.

These requests seem out of the ordinary. Then getting on the phone itself would probably put many people off. It is what I do.

If you don't ask, you don't get.

Sometimes by asking, you gain a sort of mutual respect as though part of some private member's club. When people are used to playing at that level, that is the level. It is not outrageous to them.

You forget that on a daily basis, these types of people deal with *these types of people*. They all know each other and live a little in a bubble. It was a club…a clique. It was as simple for my friend to call Harry as it was ordering pizza. You just had to be lucky, or have worked hard enough to have that contact, and then be prepared to ask. I lost that inhibition about dealing with crazy way back when I named my price for the Indian wedding in Newcastle.

If you don't ask you don't get.

Plus some celebs do like their 'giving back' moments. Gary Barlow famously tweeted that he would sing at three weddings of couples he had never met and then went on to do many more. If you don't need to work or your work life is so controlled that everything is stage-managed, but you do have a sense of humour, a heart and like to give something back, then there is a reasonable argument for understanding why there was nothing to lose in asking.

You have lost nothing if the answer is no.

Gary Barlow, the wedding singer became a viral and print sensation. We wanted to keep this particular pop star on the radar – or more importantly under the cake.

It comes simply down to this. Harry would either say yes or no.

Then, of course, if you are daft enough to brief the client that it is on and actually happening, there is that little bit of rock'n'roll doubt in you that there could be a last minute hitch, someone might get wind and that could mean paparazzi, or the star might just not fancy it. Always expect the set times to change.

Best to tell nobody and take control.

I would deliver Harry Styles personally and leave nothing to chance.

He happened to be in Leeds on the night of the party.

I sent a car so there are no hitches. I got the impression Harry liked a bit of fun.

And then it happens. He arrives on time, wheels in the cake, and leaves one young lady with a lifetime of memories that a speedboat or private jet can't buy.

There are tears. There are almost no words. Just shrieks and the vocabulary extends no further than 'Oh my God' followed by the same. Time is suspended.

Put yourself in the scene. Your life is privileged. It is your birthday. Location is amazing. You don't need to worry about picking up the tab. Your best friends are around you. You can be young and party the night away. You are set up for life and your future will be without worries. What more could make you happy? What has the power to leave you speechless, spinning in an emotional daze, shocking you into a nervous, quivering wreck? What can money *not* buy?

Ladies and gentleman, I give you Harry Styles.

And then we are done. Brief is all it takes. To linger is to outstay your welcome and make it less special. Rarity is a quality and to whisk somebody in and out, leaving them wanting more but questioning whether or not that actually happened is the stuff dreams are made of.

And I repeat – money can't buy.

As I said, those million dollar requests either costs a million dollars or nothing.

Harry didn't receive a penny.

But, of course, they come back for more and that brings repeat work and new challenges. When the same guy rings you three years later for her 21st what is the next level of expectation for him, the daughter and for you?

It is a hard act to follow but one that you will never shy away from. The reward for decades of graft and success is more of the same but greater expectation equals bigger budgets. All of that makes you smile and stimulates the creativity gene, which apart from the need to provide for the girls when they were younger, remains the motivation and inspiration for the business.

My girls in the office were always taught the golden rule.

We say yes.

'I'd like to take 40 to the top of the Eiffel Tower in Paris for dinner. Just us. Nobody else.'

No problem, I lied.

We always say yes.

So, I chartered a plane and set the wheels in motion. As you do.

The Jules Verne by Alain Ducasse was ready.

Inside the jet at a private airstrip on the outskirts of Manchester, I ripped out all the headrests and rebranded them with each of the guests' name on. Sometimes it doesn't take much to impress teenagers.

They didn't know where they were going.

Destination: Paris.

Nor, did they know they were coming back that night either.

We had them clubbing in Manchester by midnight.

A short sharp thrill of a birthday, oozing with extravagance and style – the ability to pull it off more important than feathers, flowers and food.

Sometimes people just want you to take care of it. Part of my job is allowing busy people to pass the responsibility on. They don't have time for the process, they just want the result.

The requests were becoming more and more diverse. I really don't know how this worked. Well, it is word of mouth obviously but I can't say when it kicked in – when word of mouth changed from me delivering quirky and odd to that being the minimum requirement and what people expected. Many of my clients *did* recommend me with tales of what we could achieve. Some encompassed this huge catchment area like Manchester United. Equally many of them *didn't* know each other. The development of the party and the range of requests meant literally that the sky was the limit.

It was almost as though two things were happening – as if every time we pulled something spectacular off, a website was listing it with a rhetorical challenge to top that. To my knowledge, no such platform was out there and certainly not when we started but all my clients came to me on my reputation and that was based on the ability to deliver. The part two of that is that I had long since started to believe. I went along with the hype. So, as word spread of Eiffel Towers and runaway trains, I really did both look for the challenge *and* believe that everything was possible.

In 100 years time when they have run out of plastic to keep this old dog alive, my great great grandkids will be barking at the heels of Branson's and wanting to party like it is 2099 on the International Space Station!

Naturally, if you tell a client that you have done the Paris thing or conquered the Glazers or hung up on royalty, your name-dropping becomes your CV but also they rise to the bait. You watch as their own thought process moves from 'Wow, you can do that?' as though that was way beyond their expectations to 'Right, then how about this?' which will exceed the thing that blew them away in the first place.

There is some amount of ego at play on both sides.

The corporate world in particular knows it has to better both itself and a rival. Christmas parties or annual awards can become legendary in the anecdotal history of an internal culture and when you have repeat business from these clients, the level of expectation is huge.

Take Budget Insurance, with whom I have worked for many years. *You* ring up and pay your premiums. *They* call me and I take them to Istanbul, Marrakesh, Egypt and New York to inspire, motivate and ultimately improve the service.

79

That was the level of love they wanted to show their staff but also the measurement of how the party goalposts moved year after year. Expectation in the office and internal email starts a good six months out – especially if your job is not the most exciting reason to get up in the morning. Businesses know too that they can carry a workforce on the legend of one night a year around the Christmas period. I am tuned in to that ethos.

Now, you might well recall me saying how streets ahead the USA was when I started out and that I travelled to Houston almost to research it. Two decades later and some, you would think that there was no better place set up to deliver the night of your life than a Los Angeles or a New York.

I hadn't legislated for one thing – New York was not in the land of the free!

We just viewed it with traditionally kinder eyes because we were supposed to be on the same side and spoke the same language and perceived that they did things bigger and better. Daft of me really to host my first NY event and assume that everything would run smoothly.

How many times have we all arrived at US immigration and found the process long, aggressive, exhausting and pedantic? You tick a box incorrectly on that form and you disappear two hours back to the end of the line. You overstep the *line* when you are waiting in *line*, then you are out of line. The lines are clearly marked in their eyes – except for the differing language between a line and a queue!

So how naïve was I to think I could rock up in the States with all my usual tools and tricks and lay on a gig that Budget would remember forever.

The unions were at work.

I am planning a two night function. It turns out you can't even move a table without calling in the rep. I didn't know this.

Until I tried to move a table.

That meant that NY rates as possibly the least hands-on I have ever been. I simply was not allowed to *lay hands on*.

Then I had all my suppliers to becalm too. They couldn't work and I was faced with the impossible, uncontrollable situation where the venue would recommend equivalent people in favour of my trusted entourage. Favours and backhanders at play, rules at large.

New York was rapidly becoming a 'never again'. Sad, really because Hollywood or The Big Apple would top your wish list of places to party. You see why I always bang on about control and others therefore position me as an egotist. These issues were now out of my *control* so I couldn't champion my event with confidence.

In short, I became the client of the venue and the union. That was not how it was supposed to work.

The problems were only just beginning. I was struggling to find a band because of all the paperwork it required. I had to call on a Jewish friend in New York to recommend someone who could handle such gigs. I found the brilliant incomparable Marianne Bennett Orchestra.

For the first time ever, then and since, I booked them solely on recommendations.

As a result of all the rules, I now was breaking my own. I had never seen them perform but they were in. On trust.

For logistics, America is right up there with the worst.

In Egypt, my venue is in the middle of the River Nile. I don't legislate for tide times.

The tide is in. The restaurant is in the middle of the Nile. I am in the shit. The CEO of Budget Insurance looks at me and smiles. The silence says two things – save the day…and I know you can.

He knows that I know.

I have cocked up. I mentally add tide times to the never-ending checklist locked in a compartment in my brain that every event brought a new addition to.

Tide times, for fuck's sake.

The board of directors and chairman are on a private transfer.

I know…looking back it is obvious.

You can't fight nature. But you can look it up beforehand.

He also knows me inside out and is well aware that I will find a way. The tide has dropped as the directors arrive by boat to the restaurant on the Nile.

You pay for stuff to go beyond your dreams but you also splash out for someone who can stop those moments turning into nightmares.

People look for leaders in these situations – that means your clients, their guests, your event staff and your team. Most turn their heads in my direction, some turn away.

We are in the game where everyone wants to take the credit or run a mile. I am in the business of turning heads the right way.

I have to create temporary steps using two chairs and two men.

I resolve the problem.

They see the humour!

Same company. Different city.

Istanbul, Turkey.

All my stuff is sent one day late from the UK. This is a disaster despite my rigorous timetable which I set every single time and everybody knows has to be stuck to. I don't make up dates and clocks just for the fun of it. I know what it takes so when I specify a certain schedule, I am not twiddling my thumbs and messing about. That is what needs to happen.

I land in Turkey with no flowers, no table cloths and no napkins. These are not just any flowers, table cloths or napkins. If that is what you want, don't hire me. I go the extra mile on service and quality and provide bespoke for each event.

I was not about to provide now.

This time I am in a rage.

My staff sense this and they know what to expect. Some are hyperventilating at their failure to deliver. Others are handing out beta-blockers.

I write that carefully knowing it will be misconstrued as to some kind of bullying behaviour. It is not. They know the pressure is on – doubled by being overseas and augmented by a repeat client who has standards too. They are aware the kit was sent late. They understand my anger. Their physical reaction is within themselves because they know they have messed up.

What to do? You can't abandon. Obviously. I would bloody fight on in a hurricane if I could.

You have to pull all the stops out.

I send my florist out at four in the morning. Just one brief: get everything and don't come back until you have.

She delivers.

We source 20 tablecloths too to create a magnificent dinner setting from nowhere. Then one logistic turns into another. My original gear decides to make an appearance at the time at which it is virtually no use to me. The following day.

Further note to self – allow an extra idiot day in the scheduling to compensate for local custom and as foolproof for instruction being ignored. Create deadlines and know the real deadlines.

And most of all, budget for Budget.

I have done a lot of work for Indian families. They bring big investment and big numbers. One thing I learnt even back at the Newcastle wedding is that timekeeping often goes out of the window.

I knew to lay down a marker early.

Greeting a huge party in St. Tropez, I know that I am going to struggle. I meet them personally at the airport and make them feel special before we have even met, having mailed them personalised Taylor Lynn baggage labels beforehand.

I realise that if I am going to keep a handle on the party, I have to be the face of it. There is no point sending somebody else. I distribute them into a male coach and female coach and take their luggage from them. I tell them seven o'clock in the lobby.

I really mean nine but I have learnt my lesson.

One asks me if they will still have time to go to the hairdresser. They should have asked me sooner. I bring my own on every foreign trip!

I parade the group through the streets of St. Tropez all clearly visible under my yellow flag. We wander into a group of Hells Angels.

83

There is nothing you can do about that. But I have them under control.

The guests – not the Hells Angels.

Then there is Italy.

In Venice, the entrance to our venue at the palazzo is so grim that I force the authorities to build a step on the decking up to it.

I struggle to get my flowers in and out.

Everything is taken to a central depot then distributed by barge or speedboat. These are the challenges you don't see coming. You legislate for a city built on water, then your focus would be on the stability of the event and access to it and ensuring the dryness of the guests. You do not reason for delays to couriering because of the geography of the city.

It is not the water that kills us. It is the goddam bridges in a city of hundreds. I need to get everything to the showpiece of Venice – the Grand Canal, where thousands flock every day as tourists for life memories. It is also a public highway, if you like, through which gondolas, emergency services and transport vehicles commute, entertain and patrol. Grand canal is grand central.

The only problem is my stuff won't make it.

Not unless we lie it all down flat.

Brilliant. I made the note to legislate for water. I didn't look up and factor in bridges.

Noted.

There is the lesson that whatever you accept as an engagement and wherever it to be held, you must be respectful of the cultures of your hosts and mindful of the infrastructure.

Frankly, when you are planning everything from an office in Manchester that argument sometimes just doesn't hold water.

Working the day of Princess Diana's death had been demanding – as much for the testing client as that 24 hours and the week which followed being like no other bar 9/11.

My relationship with the royals, however, extends far beyond being an observer on that tragic day.

For many years, I had been a board member of the North West Committee for The Prince's Trust.

This was the charity founded by the Prince of Wales, Prince Charles back in 1976 with the specific aim of getting vulnerable young people's lives back on track. They worked with 11-30 year olds who faced issues with their mental health, exclusion from society, education, homelessness and being taken into care, providing practical and financial support for these people, in the process raising over a billion pounds for charity and creating a platform for many hundreds of entrepreneurs to flourish from no sort of beginnings at all.

In 1976, when it started, charity was not yet an over-cooked feast. The 1980s in Britain saw a huge increase in fundraising which started with the global appeal for Ethopia through Band Aid and ended in huge campaigns for tragedies such as Hillsborough, the Bradford fire and Zeebrugge ferry disaster. As an 'industry' it grew almost alongside me and today many thousands of people work and give time for free to the charity sector and plenty of these come to me for the organisation of huge events. We expanded together and often work hand in hand.

Somehow, I had found myself getting involved. I was in so early that I was the only woman on the committee. Back then, we were rare. There were certain criteria to get on board. You had to volunteer to organise certain events – almost negotiate your way on. I could see even all those years ago that this could be hugely beneficial to both myself and the charity. Nobody really was doing what I was doing – especially in the north. I agreed to get involved.

As with all things at the start, you couldn't know where it would lead but you had a hunch that it was unlikely to be anything other than rewarding. Nearly three decades on, I can tell you that I have been to several garden parties with the Queen and am in a very small category of people who happened to turn up wearing the same Philip Treacy hat as her majesty. There really was no need for her to upstage me!

I had actually attended once before with my father in his role as a judge. I sort of had a sense of the rules and how it worked, even if dressing the same as the Queen was obviously a no-no.

You can feel in awe of occasions like this or just see it for what it is. You get your two minutes with the Queen, you are acknowledged for your efforts and you are now at the biggest networking event in the country! Honoured to be there but that was my view!

I suppose the first time you find yourself within the company of royals, it can be a little daunting – I remember being in that room with Prince Andrew overlooking Pall Mall and watching the 'servants' all choreographed and serving from the left in rhythm and mentally storing it all up as a new standard but also thinking 'Well, come on this is me and these are probably normal people underneath if you break down the barriers'.

The royals are, of course, experts at manipulating conversation. There cannot be a family who have had to make more small talk than them on the planet. Even though they are stiff upper lip British, they don't do silence and they know how to move you along.

People will find it hard to believe that there is any element of normality about them. Nor will they ever get any sympathy for trying to *be* normal. I am sure, equally, that whilst committed to their charities, this work gives them a focus and a platform when the route to the throne is a very limited one especially for somebody like Andrew. Especially now! There must be countless occasions when they are bored senseless with it all.

Take the Duke of Westminster – an inherited title that comes with privilege and obligation. I am invited to a private dinner and at the time we are both heavy smokers. You are not allowed to light up in the building. So, we both make our excuses and retreat outside for a Marlboro Light. You never see mundane moments like this.

They have a sense of humour too. Often the public don't see this because the press make them a target or make them look daft or they attempt to control back. Life is choreographed.

Over time these connections have opened so many doors.

I am invited to organise an intimate dinner at Knowsley Hall in Merseyside. It is for Bobby Arora, one of the brothers behind the B & M Bargains chain and whose wedding I organised.

When I arrive, Lord Derby is standing there in all his regalia, having just attended the swearing in for the High Sherriff of Chester.

'Sorry, I am late,' I break the ice. 'But you shouldn't have rolled out the red carpet for me.'

They hadn't of course.

'Do you know Liz?' Bobby asked.

'Of course, I do,' Lord Derby replied. 'Last time I saw her was with Prince Charles.'

It helps when people people remember you. Remaining part of the crowd is the easy part. Standing out is where you win.

But it was as late as 2016 that really put me on their map.

I got a call early in the morning.

'Can you be at Kensington Palace at 10 am tomorrow?

'Yes,' I replied.

I didn't need any more detail.

Prince William was organising his Winter Whites Ball on a Dr. Zhivago theme. Everything was going horribly wrong. They had had to relieve the existing team of their duties. The party was heading for a disaster. Could I step in?

Oh – and it is in two weeks time.

Well, the deadline was crazy. But you don't say no, do you?

'Have you booked any entertainment?' I asked.

I would see if the Swan band were available. My go to option – my ever trustworthy act of quality, always ready to deliver.

'Yes,' an assistant replied.

'OK, who?' I quizzed.

'Jon Bon Jovi and Taylor Swift.'

I would just hold for now on booking the tickets from Paris!

Wow – Jon Bon Jovi and Taylor Swift...

I continued unfazed. But it took a moment to sink in. The brain remains in the conversation but goes on partial walkabout.

They had booked two of the biggest names on the musical planet and they were inked in but the rest of the party was falling apart around them. To be honest, those two could probably boss the whole show but they wanted more. Royals – or their staff – spend huge amounts of the year organising banquets and charity dos. Yet, now they only had the talent confirmed. And I was about to sell them the Swan Band.

I hadn't considered it might be on this scale.

Despite the urgency of the deadline, I am still working to royal detail even though I need to take control. They do things their way. I watch and learn and then add a bit of me. All the place settings are rigorous – the distance between them identical to the inch. I eye the detail.

There are certain things I won't do. Many caterers put the coffee cups down on the table to speed up service. Equally they place the bread rolls next to the cutlery. I don't believe in rushing. I like people to feel the quality of the staff and feel that minutiae of detail.

I don't tolerate spelling errors. Any typos in this book are not my fault and bollockings will be ensued. If there is one thing which shows you are careless or cutting corners, it is a basic error like this. Spelling someone's name incorrectly on a place setting or table plan just says you don't care enough. Typing 'menus' with an apostrophe just lacks class. It is menus not menu's. You can hide many cock-ups during an event on the night but you can't re-do the language.

The royals of course set that bar at the highest level. Attention to deal is a whole job and not just part of one. But now *they* needed people. They just didn't have the right person before.

No time for error! But doing it my way meant doing it their way. Bar America, this is one of the few occasions where I can't call all the shots. And there is a price. Nobody works for nothing and those who say they do are lying. You charge even if it is the Royal Family. Certain protocol still had to be adhered to. When it came to sorting out my suppliers, I had to take control of that but fortunately, some of my people were already on their recommended list of people to hire.

Even at two weeks notice – for 400 people and to the standard required, this was still a tall order. I was working solely from my reputation and the perception they had of me. I was known to them of course for many years but whilst they had shook my hand and made small talk and had included me in their recognition of people who had served their charities, they had never hired me per se.

Until now.

I do not meet Prince William or Kate until the night. She is heavily pregnant with Prince George so is unable to attend.

William steals the show.

Literally. Steals it.

The stage is white. I have built a wintery wonderland.

'Just maybe the karaoke kid could come up and sing it for you,' Jon Bon Jovi takes to the mic.

'I can't fly helicopters or ride motorcycles like you…

A couple of words…'

The crowd is urging the prince to the stage.

'Tommy used to work on the docks…you're gonna come up for the chorus…'

It gets louder and louder.

'Take that long walk up here,' the Bon Jovi frontman is half singing half commentating.

The future king emerges, hand in hand with Taylor Swift.

Jon Bovi Jovi is strumming, violinist to his left. Taylor Swift is swaying slightly and the Duke of Cambridge is Dad-dancing to his side, fake re-adjusting his bowtie to make himself looking cool. They both roar the chorus while Jon bon Jovi beams a smile.

The audience erupts.

Putty in hands.

Cameras are clicking everywhere.

This is the money shot.

At a private event.

Whatever else happens, this is the moment everyone will remember. And that is my job done. Every event must have its take away and tell element. You must give birth to a legend. This is that moment.

William and Jon Bon Jovi hug then the future king escorts Taylor Swift off the stage. Ringmaster Jonathan Ross returns to the stage to urge more.

The clips go viral immediately.

An event that few outside of it knew was even happening is now an internet sensation.

The Telegraph have footage. BBC Breakfast call. The next day I am on the breakfast TV sofa.

We pulled it off. Living on a wing and a prayer.

18 You Don't Bring Me Flowers Any More

My ex had been right about one thing.

'Don't go 50:50 with Dianne,' I had never forgotten him saying.

Of course, by this point, it looks as though I can't hold down any bloody relationship but actually that isn't true because in the background of failed marriages and business divorces stood a team of suppliers, designers, manufacturers and caterers with whom I had worked for years and would continue to do so.

At different times in life, people want different things and at various stages of the evolution of the business, somebody always wants to go their own way. Someone turns your head, ambition kicks in, the grass is always greener, life gets in the way. All that...

As much it suited me to work with the Seawards and then go alone, the same was true of Dianne.

This time, I really was ready to go solo.

The Taylor Lynn Company would in effect be just the Taylor bit. But the name would stand and hey, everyone needs a little TLC, don't they?

I wasn't precious.

Well – not about that anyway.

It had taken me a long time to get here. Several decades. Even now I knew that you were only as good as your last gig but my mind was strong and my focus resilient. I knew the moment was right for us to go our separate ways and that I would never go into a partnership again.

It was as much a reflection on me as anything else. Plus, it was time.

I guess my confidence was for once complete. Of course, I lived with that paranoia that it could all collapse tomorrow and the more money you earned the greater the feeling it was not enough and you might lose it. That was in my genetics *but* in my head, I was ready.

Yet, something clearly was deeper than that because on the day that I bought Dianne out, I headed straight out of the solicitors and to the car showroom. My guilty pleasure, in the wings since starting in business was ready for me.

I drove home in my brand new Porsche Carrera. I love cars. I adore driving. It was one box ticked.

I know it spelt success, independence, contentment and onwards and upwards. It drew a line at least in my mind.

I was often building images for clients in the corporate side of my work. Every Manchester United party had to better the previous one. Word of each Budget Insurance bash had to spread to its competitors. But, I was no different too. In my role, I had become public because of the profile of many of my clients. That meant that I had to think about my image too.

So this was my statement and I made no excuses.

My God, Dad would finally approve.

The only danger with being a bit flash of course was just walking that fine line between playing the part and fitting in with your clientele without leaving them thinking that you had bought your lifestyle with their money. You don't want to be too in your face!

There had been a lot to sort – the business and our relationship looked so different from where it started. Fundamental differences always existed. I was very much a 6 am to 6 pm worker, Dianne often preferred an 11-8 day. Nothing wrong with that but we became less and less in synch and I know that I wanted to take the business in a different direction.

But it wasn't just *the business*. By the end of the road, there were several businesses. We owned two properties together. I sold my share and could only shrug years later when Dianne sold them on herself for a considerable return. That is the way it goes. There was also TLC – the table linen company! – which we had started after a Caribbean themed event meant we were making hundreds of lime green chair covers and table cloths and then went on to produce dozens of amazing different fabrics. We went to Germany to buy red and gold plates to create the picture and ended up selling the business back to the people who made the linen for us.

The business and the businesses had both grown so significantly that I had begun to wonder why I had gone 50:50 in the first place. That though is a reflection at the end of the process where the brain dismisses where you were when you started. Mindful of never really receiving promised dividends from the Seaward Organisation, I think my belief had been strong when Dianne and I started but my confidence was low.

Perhaps, if I had been ruthless at the outset and asked to go 70:30, I might have persevered more with the relationship but if it weren't for Dianne, I would never have invested at all in property. She had been the tough one and given me the confidence to take a punt.

Whatever the theme or the occasion, we bounced off each other without really needing much dialogue. In short, there was almost a silent understanding and we cleaned up in Manchester as a result.

Nothing by this stage phased us – if you wanted a Moroccan tent, no problem. That Waldorf spirit never left me. We clearly had different skills – mine was buying in what we needed and hers was to make it happen. That contrast was always a strength but of course, it often meant our own focuses and aspirations went separate ways.

But, it was a totally different separation from London. Then, with two young children, I was slightly panicky at losing a monthly salary despite my frustrations. Now, I felt ready and set up to go alone. I had moved on in life and whilst Manchester had become competitive in an industry which had not started when I began, I knew that I would continue to flourish without this time needing to question it was viable employment.

I would not have been as successful without Dianne. Much more laid back and stable than me. I valued her as a friend, and never one for regrets, every single day I have plenty of reasons to wish we were still close.

But, the truth is that from my point of view, it *felt* like it was my business, so I made it my business to go solo and, with my team around me, stay solo.

I simply moved from one end of Deansgate in Manchester to the other and never looked back.

It was not lost on me though that the two single most influential women in my career – Lorraine Seaward and Dianne both shared the same birthday.

Perhaps we were meant to meet and maybe it was inevitable that we would all move on.

19 Full House

Dianne's legacy to me is rich.

Sometimes people arrive in your life to take you to the next stage – like crossing a pool of water on stepping stones, one hand leading the other across.

Dianne threw me my life jacket when I was no longer seaward and then saw me safely onto dry land. Quite possibly, I was always destined to set sail alone.

Clearly, she gave me the belief to leave London, go with her and then ironically, to part with her. Creatively, we shone together though often apart. Those two elements remain rooted in me today. Professionally, my self-belief is second to none. My production values are better than they have ever been.

But there is another side to our relationship which has been crucial to my stability but also underlines that it might just look like I organise a few parties and what a job that is etc but actually I am an entrepreneur and the event is the icing on the cake from a background of public relations and fashion. Essentially, I am a business women.

It is easy for cake and candles to hide that fact.

Dianne helped mould that. She led me towards property. Without her, I probably would have only bought the house that I lived in – not the dozen or so that I ended up investing in.

I was always conscious that entertainment was a young person's game, though here I am still in it. I knew that people were catching me up and all it took was one party, one magazine cover, one big commercial relationship to fall sour, one new kid on the block with social media skills to knock me for six and suddenly that phone might not ring any more.

You may well perceive from the clients I detail that this is paranoid and that surely I didn't have to chase work. Today, as it stands, that is true. You never know, though, what tomorrow brings.

So, that same survival instinct – earn your own money with a Saturday job, feed your kids and bring them up alone –

quite clearly remained whether it was 1989 or 2019. No amount of security would satisfy. Paranoia was good for business.

But, of course, you have to find another string to your bow if there is no business and that is where the housing market came in. From the moment Dianne and I bought our first property to work out of, I promised myself to put every spare bit of cash into housing. We begun with both of us buying half of half of the building we were in and then picked up commercial premises for our linen business. My husband and accountant asked me what the hell I was doing when I bought into the TLC headquarters. Hindsight is a wonderful thing. On this occasion I was definitely correct to go with my gut feeling.

Next, I picked up a flat in London. I admit I got lucky with some investments on one occasion picking up a house for £40,000 and selling it relatively quickly for £120,000. Mostly, I would the money back in.

My purchases were random. Often I would just google upcoming areas with great facilities around them – the obvious stuff like schools and public transport where I can make a 7 or 8 % return on my income – and then I would buy, rarely visiting my purchase. Some, to this day, I have never seen.

That meant, of course, that you would ride the ups and downs of the housing market – recessions would come along once a generation and 2007's Credit Crunch meant that house prices stalled or dropped and nobody was buying but that didn't matter because I wasn't really that bothered about selling. Occupation and rental income were king.

It has been an undoubted success story and I would not have been here without Dianne. Roger's discouragement should have rung alarm bells at the time.

That desire to be self-sufficient and not dependent on a single source made my character vulnerable. That bred an almost OCD nature that meant I couldn't stop. I never could and I doubt I can.

I became addicted to my own angst. I would never know how far or how high. The next level always drove me on without any sense of perspective that I had 'succeeded' or had 'more than enough' to support me.

96

It is important to understand that this is not greed that motivates. I do, after all have a nice life where I can go to my retreat in Turkey and lie next to Kate Moss, both of us cucumberred up to the eyeballs though her looking a slightly younger model. That fear of *not* being self-sufficient means that I have no understanding of what a sum of money represents. I am transparent with fees and make no excuses and I earned well but that paranoia always haunts me. I am going to need more at some point.

I back my own judgement – except in my personal life. My business relationships have been a lot more successful than my own ones. I can make decisions quickly and mostly correctly for other people *but* my love life has been a disaster.

There is frankly little I can do about this. It is how I am built.

That makes me very hard on myself. Other people see that as arrogance. But it is fear. I still wake every morning knowing the business could fail. The properties remain occupied. At least, I have a Plan B.

And you really do not know what lies ahead – any business can go to the wall. If once upon a time there was no industry such as this then equally it is possible to return to that mentality. You just don't know. Brexit awaits as I write and whilst it is highly likely that the status quo prevails, nobody has any true notion of its impacts. If companies re-locate or go under, you guarantee one thing – the first budget to be slashed is staff entertainment and corporate hospitality.

Everything is constantly changing. What you once took for granted can no longer be counted on.

Manchester United themselves, one of my best and biggest clients are still not the team they were several years now into the post Sir Alex Ferguson era. Every football club goes through cycles. It is unlikely to imagine a day where they will not have huge demand but football is very volatile and a new owner and manager can bring many things. I never take that relationship for granted.

These are the parameters by which you play and which control the angst. The big dos for the wealthy clients will always

97

remain. Their excessive wealth generally is already made and overrides the economic climate. But, as long-standing as many of those relationships have been with me, they won't use you every time and they can't use you at all if your own business goes under because the 'bread and butter' has all but dried up.

Because of my drive and this fear, I have never been in that position since I started in the 80s. But I carry it every day, and that is most definitely a good fear to avoid complacency whilst of course remaining a terrible monkey on your back when it comes to switching off. That is why you will understand from me that I see every chance meeting on a train etc is another door opening. I don't have time to stop or see it any other context. Everybody needs a party at some point.

Equally, regardless of the economic outlook in the country, there are people snapping at my heels and somebody will blow me out of the market at some point. It is as simple as buying a car. The manufacturer brings out a new model, leaving the previous one just looking a little older and more tired.

You may well ask therefore if it would be easier to just sell the business. I have had discussions over the years. You don't have to be a genius to work out though that, as much as I need and love my team and give them every opportunity to 'invest' their own careers in the company, if I am not part of it then there might not necessarily be anything to sell. Plus walking away denies me that creative buzz.

Dabbling in property – and seeing the results – of course then makes you think what might be next in life. It is, to a degree, gambling. Success spurs you on.

I have toyed many times with opening a bar. That would be a dream come true. If somebody gave me a million, then I might consider it but I am not about to throw my own money at it. I would quite happily be a maître d and I would love to bullshit my way through a night on the music but I have to draw the line at getting financially involved.

Remember – I have staged so many events that I know that scene inside out. I get the margins and I see that for many there is no trade Monday to Thursday and I don't know how you can run a business like that.

As a consultancy, I will make you the best bar possible. But you have to run it and I am not putting my money there! I am not trying to be clever. I am trying to get a pension.

Thanks to Dianne, I chose the property path and my portfolio remains pretty full.

To date, my worst investments are only in men.

20 Moscow – In A Hurry

A full portfolio of clients need not know the ins and the outs. The show must go on. Divorce in the March from Dianne. Champions League Final in the May. The show does go on.

When you are re-structuring and re-establishing your confidence solo, you need your clients who have been with you for years. Knowing they will be there still gives you that belief. The last thing you want is your clients who have been with you for years ringing you at two weeks notice!

In the same way that I had become date aware after the Remembrance Day lock-in, I knew that May was always the end of the football season. For United that brought expectation.

I still knew nothing about the game but I did grasp the fact that Manchester United were normally heading towards a league title, an FA Cup, or very occasionally, the final stages of the elite Champions League.

2008 posed the biggest challenge yet in over 20 years.

United were to play Chelsea. The already pre-determined venue whoever got there was Moscow. That meant you were looking at a stadium of capacity of close to 70,000 fans all converging from the UK, plus many without tickets.

And that is before you factor in the couple of hundred personnel involved with the clubs.

You would never get much more than a fortnight's notice for such a showpiece because there was no guarantee you would progress past the semi-final. Worse – Manchester United had already sent out a representative from the club with a view to doing what I do and had been quoted around well over the odds per head.

The Russians had seen everyone coming. Flights and hotels were going through the roof. All roads led to the Russian capital.

I make my first trip to Moscow just ten days before the final itself. It doesn't get much tighter than that, nor give you room to negotiate. Heavens above if you then got into any bureaucratic nightmare nor could you get the freight plane in time.

Anyone with money of a Chelsea or Manchester United allegiance was heading there and paying through the odds. There was extra spice too in that the owner of Chelsea Football Club is Roman Abramovich, the Russian billionaire.

As ever time was running out. I had no cards to deal.

I managed to get it down considerably, returns having met expectation.

Stage one covered.

You do what you have to do to get it down in price.

It is a ball ache and a challenge but I have to win.

And it's Russia.

I order in black glass tables and have a bespoke bar all to be made from scratch on site.

I rip up the meat stew menu on offer at the hotel. By the time this game finishes nobody is going to want to eat that. For the global TV audience, the game kicks off at 2245 local time for Heaven's sake. I toss it out and instigate breakfast with salmon, caviar and eggs.

I have 22 set builds, a production team and an aircraft of freight. You are looking at twelve months work to pull this off – and I have to get visas for the lot of them.

In ten days.

Plus the band – the band are coming in from Paris. With all their kit too. They have by now performed for Manchester United for many years. There is no party without The Swan.

It is a 'challenge' from start to finish – old school Soviet Union. Up there with New York.

We land in Moscow on Sunday morning. Four days to build.

By evening, there is no sign of the freight plane.

Customs are holding it. For no obvious reason. Nor do they give us any explanation at all. The cold war is back!

First thoughts are that Roman Abranovich is behind this.

He wants to make a statement. Chelsea must win. Anything to disrupt the Manchester United charge is fair game.

Everything is in that hangar hidden inside the airport – red roses from Holland and 20,000 flowers wilting away, yards of red-pleated fabric, French horns and drum kits. No plane, no party.

I don't sleep at night, realising that plane could be there forever until people forget about it. By 3 pm local time on the Wednesday of the match, I still have no plane.

I resort to walking around with a bumbag of cash, prepared to bribe anybody. This is a different game. I start to befriend the general manager who is of somewhat dubious sexuality. I start to flirt with her. There is this girl hanging around the hotel who seems to have some connection to authority.

These are my only hopes.

I am introduced to a contact who gives me some sort of ridiculous reason for the delay like the plane is overweight. If so, then they have made their point.

I have only hours left before kick-off, albeit at that late hour.

I rescue my aircraft in the nick of time and am further assisted by the match going to extra time and penalties. John Terry has the chance to win the game for Chelsea but slips and misses. United win 6-5. The game finished at 1-1 after the 120 minutes. The longest and most draining of days was now heading into the earliest of mornings.

Nobody needed stew after that. Naturally, I had been in one all day but no-one was any the wiser. Not for the first time, the band are getting ready without a soundcheck or their gear – definitely the last time I say yes to Russia!

It drained the life out of me. I can tell you I do not undertake any such trip without weighing everything and logging anything. I even have paperwork for the paperwork. I leave nothing to chance but you can't legislate for jobsworths or a little bit of local politics. Who knew how the wheels of corruption and influence grinded in a place like Russia.

I confessed in the early hours to the Commercial Director of Manchester United that there had been the odd hurdle to overcome and could he get me out of there as quickly as possible.

He put me on the United plane home.

Oddly, my £38,000 hire of freight plane did not have the same problems leaving the country as getting in.

In fact, if I am ringing Manchester Airport and I tell them it is for Manchester United, the floodgates open – everybody wants to help – and obviously to carry this off at ten days notice you need everything to go to plan and to pull the odd string.

In Russia, it was they who were pulling mine.

Never again.

Never ever again.

From Russia with love. Not!

I knew that Dianne and I would both be watching each other for a while – not just in terms of how I was going on my own or if she was set free too but those areas where we once held a shared interest. How would that property we had bought together thrive in time for example?

You would always take an interest from afar. Equally you had to crack on.

I never set out to make a statement but if I was to really go it alone this time, I had to back myself to go bigger and better than ever.

I knew deep down that word of my parties had always spread and that was how I got repeat and new bookings but everybody was aware that with me in total control now, I would be looking to go off the scale again.

Enter John Cauldwell.

Google him today and you will see extreme wealth next to his name – estimations in the billions.

In 2009 I knew him as the Phones 4U guy. With his brother, and from their roots in Newcastle-Under-Lyme, Staffordshire they had over 600 stores at the birth of the mobile phone era.

His daughter was turning 21.

She was a huge fan of *The Wizard of Oz* prequel, *Wicked* – that was the brief.

Oh – and Diana Ross was coming.

Budget…optional! If you like, we are on a completely different network.

I begin dealing with Diana Ross's people. You can never be quite sure what you are getting in agreement and what will materialise on the day. All I knew is not to look at her, get an ironing lady and an iron board, build a green room and fill it with specific furniture. They are the demands.

I am not allowed to look at Diana Ross. She the singer of the hit *Reflections* didn't want to see mine.

I was being out-*diva*d!

I have to build a green room before I build the set. Just so you are sure, I use the term green room in its entertainment meaning. Not because I had overdosed on *Wicked*.

But actually, I did. This is part of the job that nobody sees. If you want a *Wicked* party, there is only one professional thing to do if you are preparing properly. I had to find where the show was on and take myself off to see it for myself.

Nobody wants an unhappy artist an hour before they are due on. A green room she will have. The truth is that you will have little to do with them before the night – the key is the people around her. She is pretty much out of my hands.

So long as I don't look at her.

Afterwards, people weren't really talking about Diana Ross. That was where the excitement lay for me.

Instead, the stage blew them away. And here lies the challenge. There was some element of anticipation before this do of what it might hold. The guests knew that John would push the boat out and that the evening might have a feel to it on a par with Disney production values. You still have the element of surprise on the night, however.

As a rule, I hated ventriloquist dummies but I did want some sort of animated witch that would speak and move – its head nodding. So that is what I built down a 30 metre walkway.

At the end of welcome drinks, the clock strikes midnight. The wall drops revealing The Yellow Brick Road. The tinman emerges – ahead a three feet high red glitter shoe supports dining tables as the scarecrow is suspended above against a backdrop of green and black.

Nobody could forget that. That is what would touch them in the morning and whatever happened after, no-one could remember.

Except John – he knew that I had delivered and delivered in style. Every gig is an advert and a potential renewal. Those in the room looked me up and John and his family earmarked me in for more.

Before I knew it, I was working for them again – John's 60th where he booked out Blenheim Palace, world heritage site and hundreds of years of history at the heart of Oxfordshire. If you could, you could!

Of course, the logistics between building the yellow brick road and working on listed buildings is one hell of a gulf! Without setting out to test me, when John booked me for his big birthday bash, I knew I had to better myself in totally different surroundings.

Here was a man who was powerful and his attention to detail on a par with my anal nature.

This time the theme was the 1920s. I built a two-tier marquee with a sweeping staircase – fit for a royal. Well, in fact, an ex-royal. The former Duchess of York, Sarah Ferguson was in the house!

John was to come down the stairs to the sound of the Proclaimers hit '500 miles'. To be fair to him, as rousing a reception as it would bring him, he had come a lot further from his roots in Staffordshire. The daft thing is, if we could get Diana Ross, we could have easily got Charlie and Craig from the band to sing him in.

And right then as he descended, I would have done anything to present a diversion.

To the crescendo of the final chorus, I suddenly spied one of my tables collapsing. Some idiot hadn't checked to see if the legs were locked in. I was seething inside, looking for somebody to blame.

My team were brilliant but this was rubbish.

And then I found that person.

It was me.

I had messed up.

I got to work straightaway knowing I had limited time before John might notice.

But he had. Thankfully, it was only his own attention to detail that spotted it whilst everyone else partied on. He is also smart enough to understand that sometimes it is not about the pickles that you get yourself into but how you recover.

You don't get to his level without realising that people make mistakes and those errors define character.

For me, it couldn't have gone more wrong. I was mortified.

Afterwards we joked, and I knew that you had to keep your balls about you dealing with people like John. He didn't want bullshit.

'Fucking hell,' I said. 'It could only happen to me.'

Then, I told him straight.

'You need to go more lightly down the stairs.'

'What do you do then?' the suave Irishman purred in my direction.

It was not as though I could ask him the same question back.

'I am an event and party planner,' I told him.

'Oh, I am 50 in December,' he beamed.

And on that polite small talk, our friendship was formed. This was now March 2009.

'You do realise that you are not going to leave here today until you've agreed to let me do your party, don't you?

I trapped him.

That was of course how I worked. If you can't get them there and then in the moment, you might not get them at all. Of course, you could try to bulldoze your way through a wall of PAs and receptionists but if you didn't seize the moment, it would leave you well behind. The moment gave you the chance to get past the PA.

He was, of course, a regular at Manchester United so he would have seen plenty of examples of what I have done over the years without necessarily making the association. Now, as luck or tactical seating arrangements would have it, I find myself sat next to him at a club lunch.

He is Eamonn Holmes.

It gets better. His wife, Ruth Langsford, and I share the same birthday. I always looked to signs like this. Just like Lorraine and Dianne previously, and Jackie Adams. It was an ice breaker.

I now have the entire lunch to make sure both become my clients. It could open a wealth of possibilities.

The fact of the matter is that he is charming and we connected, so it was not a case of me saying that I know how to get what I want and there was no way he was getting out of there alive – though that was true too.

He is also very genuine and so when I left with his phone number, I knew the gig was in the bag. I just had to be pro-active and put a few ideas into his head.

So, I did.

I turned the dance floor into a football pitch and lined the tables with astro turf, each bearing a match ball. Unfortunately, Eamonn had written a speech referring to all the place names at the table.

We hadn't placed any names on the tables.

I messed up.

Eamonn, of course, can talk his way calmly and charmingly out of a box – exactly the same demeanour, poise, professionalism and wit that you see on the box. He is that person. He is one of the few who can walk into a room and know everybody's name and still recall it years later if he is back at the same venue. He is a master at work but it never looks like work.

He just sailed on through but it left me wondering if he would book me again. I knew we could laugh our way out of it.

'You are going to have let me do your wedding now you know,' I joked but of course, never joking at all.

I would always use that forward humour and cheek to make a casual pitch and plant the seed.

Eamonn was a match for me:

'I guarantee you at least an interview with Ruth,' he smiled back.

'Ruth, I promise you that I will do your next wedding after Eamonn for free!' I replied.

And I got the gig.

He could have picked anyone in the world but he was true to his word and character – as was the wedding. No personal exuberance and not littered with an obscene amount of showbiz characters…the actress Sue Johnston and broadcasters Jeremy Kyle and Gloria Hunniford amongst the guests.

But it was Christopher Biggins who stole the show!

Almost nobody knew what was coming. I was kept pretty much in the dark. There were a few whispers amongst my production crew that the loveable joker was up to something and to just go with it.

This was not my style.

But what the hell do you say to Biggins?!

Nobody foresaw what happened next.

Cabaret time.

Susan Boyle enters the stage.

She had become a worldwide sensation in the third series of *Britain's Got Talent* in 2009 when from nowhere she absolutely smashed *I Dreamed A Dream*.

When I say 'from nowhere' so much of that is to do with pre-conception. She walked on to the stage nervously. She didn't look a star. People made assumptions about he because of the way she appeared. By the morning after her audition had been shown she was clocking up millions of hits on You Tube and American TV was calling. Simon Cowell was definitely seeing pound signs.

The unlikeliness of her stage presence against the phenomenal voice took the world by storm. She was also ridiculed for that appearance.

But in 2009, she was massive.

She did not play Eamonn's wedding.

It was Biggins in disguise bringing the house down dressed as her then later leading everyone in a spontaneous version of *Riverdance*.

And every wedding has its unplanned moment.

Biggins looked better as Boyle than Boyle did.

From this moment, the three of us struck up a friendship that lasts to this day and would spill over into work. And I still speak to Biggins! Still no word from Boyle.

Sometimes, I would work with them and on others I wouldn't. I would always see Eamonn at Manchester United and our paths would across again as he would recommend me for other work too.

We gave *Hello* one of their big wedding specials. The venue, The Elvetham, a 19th century grand Hampshire hotel received publicity few could dream of.

In time, I would learn how loyal he was to me when my own life hit the buffers. For now, I was more that happy he would tell everybody that when Liz Taylor calls, you always answer.

And as you would expect, I rang a lot!

Once upon a time, ITV decided to make a TV show detailing all the extravagances of the Premier League wife. The year is 2002 – a decade on from the new money first arriving into football when Sky revolutionised the game.

Footballers' wives.

They tapped into something that really was just beginning through the fame of David Beckham's wife Victoria and the circus around everything Beckham, and this commodity which probably peaked around the Germany 2006 World Cup by which point the word 'Wags' was in daily use and the *wives and girlfriends* were making as much noise and news as the players on the pitch.

Hindsight is a wonderful thing and we know a lot more now about our old friend the charmer Sven. It seems to fit his character and his ladies man image that when England's 'Golden Generation' rocked up to storm football's showpiece only to succumb in the usual manner, it was on his watch that the women all went too – famously reported to be dancing on the tables in the team resort of Baden Baden, a modest German retreat with relaxing hot springs.

Victoria was the queen of all Wags. Cheryl Cole was not far behind. Scroll forward to today and I present the case for Coleen Rooney versus Rebekah Vardy. Even today where the wives of the players live in luxury – scroll on to the TV show *Real Housewives of Cheshire* – Wag culture is part of the mainstream now but nothing came close to that swelling of scrutiny (except the dermal filler in their lips) that began with the original TV show and concluded with Sven's dismissal as England manager.

Have I met and worked for people who fit this description? Of course!

And some who don't – compare this era to that of wonderfully modest and Marina Dalglish. Kenny, a warm, witty Scot and the star of his generation alongside Kevin Keegan. Marina, his rock in the *background,* a cancer sufferer who fought and rose again to engage my services because she wanted to give back.

Believe me too that whilst Kenny – King Kenny – was an absolute star on the pitch and carried himself with incredible dignity post Hillsborough in 1989 when he was now manager, the wealth that even today's average players accumulate absolutely dwarves what greats like him received in their era.

Footballers do have pressured lives and are under constant scrutiny even when not playing. You are never too far away from a neighbour snooping and taking a picture of you putting your bins out. That neighbour might live a mile and half down your driveway but you know the score.

The money means that they don't want for anything and they buy exactly what they want when they want it. Their wives do not need to work – some do and others have started very successful brands sometimes using their husband's wealth and on the back of that success. I am mindful not to tar them all with the same brush but I observe that when you have it all on a plate for you, one key element to founding a new enterprise is missing.

There is no element of risk and no consequence for failure. They could throw a million at something and wake up to see it has crashed and burned and their life won't change other than a few people might laugh at them a little.

In short, we are in a different league.

That means when it comes to parties, this is also the market to be in. Quite often, the player signs it off and the wife or girlfriend does the detail. The numbers could be anything – making a show and cutting a magazine deal whilst surpassing the previous publication's party are sometimes at the forefront of their aspirations.

For others, it can be simply making a statement. When the Beckhams really came under the cosh after the Rebecca Loos story, that is a good time to do a friendly publication with editorial control to just keep the united front on track.

So, unsurprisingly, outside of the more structured world of corporate Manchester United where I was working for the team and the brand, individuals began to ring me more and more.

Let's start with the Lord of the Manor.

Djibril Cisse, the French striker, signed for Liverpool in 2004. In a mixed career, he both broke his legs twice and went on to win the Champions League and play for his national team at two World Cups. Of course, I do not remember him for anything on the pitch and yes, you are right, I had to get my assistant to look up his career stats!

Naturally, off the pitch is where I come in. Proof that newspapers will print anything and that footballers can fit that stereotype that the TV show was peddling, Cisse found himself in the news within his first year at Anfield.

He had bought himself the *title* of Lord of the Manor of Frodsham. Well, technically he bought the nine acre estate, Ridge Manor House in Cheshire for a couple of million but with it came the title when the vendors moved on to Malta.

As I have just done to illustrate the point, it got written up as though he had paid himself into British ancestry. The truth is that the title came with the property – just like the six bedrooms, four bathrooms, stables, indoor pool and chauffeur's cottage. They really could have set *Footballer's Wives* here.

I do not even know how he was put in touch with me – the phone was ringing all the time by this point. Suddenly, I am being taken to a game in a massive blacked out white Hummer, which at this time was a particular choice of vehicle for the wealthy. Then, in my inappropriate navy suit, I am heading into The Kop, clutching my Chanel bag. I am not about to fall into any stereotyping of Scousers as I would have felt the same anywhere but I clung to it and I did not expect to exit later still with it in tow! In fact, my perception of the home end changed slightly. The awe with which the fans greeted one of their stars arriving was new territory. That hustle and bustle and crowd mentality outside any British football ground soon subsided as we approached. The Red Sea literally parted as they cleared the way for the Lord's entry.

Ask me the score of that match and I have no idea. I only cared about one thing. I still have my bag!

I often get asked if I ever got so far down the line with a client and then it didn't happen. Well now, the Lord had a lady and that proved to be part of the problem.

She wanted to do it her way. Not mine.

Big mistake, obviously.

He was to marry in a red suit – the venue was a Warner Resort in Wales. It was a totally bizarre un-football type choice and I do not do bizarre unless I invent it.

Unfortunately, or fortunately, depending on your viewpoint, in time the Lord got rid of the Lady.

Believe it or not, some footballers were actually human. Believed to be *super-human* on the pitch and albeit in the confines of their huge palaces, some would still open the door in their pants.

That's for you, Steven Gerrard!

I was asked to visit to plan their house warming party on The Wirral. I was all ready to take down the brief but Stevie G was standing there in them. I have seen many successful people wobble to jelly in front of their icons. It was a potential banana skin but I was ready for anything and everything. As history has since shown, it was Stevie who slipped up when Liverpool were on the way to the title against Chelsea in 2014.

You just have to be very cool about it all, haven't you?!

Much later came Ronald Koeman, the Dutch legend but then briefly the Everton manager. Whilst I had worked with many clients around the world, much of has grown from Manchester and Manchester and Merseyside don't really do each other.

Though, we were in the bubble of football and Ronald Koeman could have had no knowledge of who I was or what I did, as smart a guy as he is. Chance, of course, played a part. Never under-estimate what you are invited to.

I had been asked to attend a dinner as a guest of Chanel at the Manchester Art Gallery. His wife Bartina is standing alone, looking miserable. Over the years, this scenario would repeat itself. My radar would always hone in on stylish well-dressed and label-conscious women isolated at events.

So we got talking. Then she booked me. Could I do their daughter's 21st on New Year? Obviously, I could.

I don't think the boss really had much to do with it and the older Dutch footballer's wife came with much less pretence and a whole lot more real world than their younger counterparts. Football was now booking me regularly.

There is also the side which many people never see. The current Manchester City team have set themselves very high standards and do not generally make an exhibition of themselves around town. I recently saw a tweet from my friend Gary Neville who owns a fair chunk of the area and is hugely connected. He essentially said that he is out and about in Manchester all the time and he doesn't know where they hang out.

This is another development in the story of the WAG. We have few foreign famous wives and girlfriends who court the public glare. The 'role' is traditionally a British one and even though the Premier League with all its richness was always able to import the cream of foreign talent, the number of overseas stars playing is now sky high. Some successful British clubs often do not feature a British player – City can be amongst them.

A different culture has therefore arrived in British football through the class of foreign purchase and the hiring of foreign managers. The latter have a different perspective and quite often bring their culture and training staff from previous clubs.

All the key influences amongst winners and success is, for the most part, coming from overseas. England still has star names but most people probably can't name the England captain Harry Kane's wife or indeed many of his team's.

I make this point because it is really important to show balance here and to underline the gulf between that TV show, the 2006 World Cup and the perception of what a footballer's party might be.

That is where the former City player Yaya Toure comes in. Part of the Barcelona team which won six trophies in a calendar year in 2009, he had more then earned his stripes by the time he swapped Spain for Manchester in 2010.

Most importantly, he had over 100 caps for his country, the Ivory Coast and represented them in six Africa Cup of Nations tournaments.

He had moved around the world, as his younger brother would too and lived his dream of playing top flight football but never ever forgot his roots.

In almost the second wave of imports in to the Premier League, scouts were seriously looking at Africa. Yaya was treated as a king there.

Chance, once again, played a part in our meeting.

I would regularly take the London train from Wilmslow in Cheshire and over time would be picked up by the same taxi driver. In fact, I pretty much lived on that train for a while to the degree that I was on first name terms with the platform attendant. Hey, I would chat to anyone. You don't know where it would lead.

I must have more upgrades than anyone on the trip to London – forever turning up with the wrong ticket to be greeted by the same guy and the same words.

'It's Liz Kardashian,' he would smile.

And so it would continue for years.

When the cabbie wasn't on the station run, he begun working for Yaya and as we all know taxi drivers like to tell you who they have had in the back of their cab…he told me he had the main man. In fact, he had picked him up so frequently that he was now on call 24/7 to the family.

And it was a family affair when I met them on my driver's recommendation. His wife was there and his wife's family lived with them too. They spent much of the time picking my brain on fashion. They had become immersed in a label-conscious world. He was a hero but humility was his middle name – one of several African footballers believed to have sent much money back home to build infrastructure against the backdrop of poverty.

Would I organise a modest fundraiser for him to coincide with his anointment as African footballer of the Year?

Yes – of course.

Would the entire squad turn up in support?

117

No – some who did hadn't realised it was black tie. A few of the others just didn't show. I don't know why.

A curious kind of envy or just a lack of awareness?

Instinct told me this was big when I picked up the phone. Of course, the phone rings hundreds of times a week and now, generally, you have people's numbers stored. But, in 2011 people were still ringing landlines, and indeed today if you don't have my number that is obviously your first port of call.

Sometimes, you have a sixth sense that this is a call you have to take. I can't really put my finger on why – it is just gut feeling accumulated over the years.

Often, there can be a cageyness at the other end. Equally, brashness too. Almost without fail in these scenarios, nobody has a normal telephone voice. This, obviously reflects the wariness and nervousness of them not quite sure what they are getting or lays down a marker to the confidentiality required when dealing with wealth or fame. My daughters call mine my London voice!

It is a game on both sides. I always back my radar when the call comes in. You learn what to ask and what not to. Listening is key.

'I am in town for a meeting with three companies and you are one of those who has been recommended to me,' she began.

This was a good opening line, whether true or not. Being seen to being in demand meant you were in control. I knew these tricks.

'I'm walking up to the Hilton at ten,' she said.

'Ah, you must be walking up from Great John Street...' I butted in, trying to connect, knowing it was the nearest to Manchester's Deansgate.

What I was actually saying was two things. I am listening and understanding who you are...and crucially, I am about to intercept.

She was telling me she couldn't get a room at Great John Street. It was full.

I knew I could swing that. I could get a room anywhere!

119

'Give me five,' I said. 'If I sort the room will you meet me at The Hilton?'

I was already negotiating.

I just didn't know with whom or for what.

'You have a deal,' she replied.

I called her back within a few minutes, having found that elusive room. The hotel knew me well enough to not mess about. If I couldn't give them a name or a reason, it didn't matter. They did it on trust too and knew that at some point, the favour would repay itself. Not everything involves money changing hands. Even in this day and age.

I called her back.

What is the worst thing that can happen? I get a free room and it comes to nothing. What have we lost?

It gives the client confidence – you are swift and efficient. You have already delivered what you said you would.

'Who are you, by the way?' I asked.

I can still hear the response today.

'I am Gary Barlow's PA.'

Well, there you go. That is what comes from having a hunch, working blind on instinct and treating everybody with top drawer service even when you have nothing to go on.

I suppose, looking back on the conversation now, this is the point where the deal was closed. Obviously I had to deliver when we met, and then again at the do but I remain supremely confident that if you can get past the gatekeeper, the keys to the castle are yours.

And so it was.

Plus – this was not just Gary Barlow. It was bigger than that. This was also *Children In Need*, the annual BBC appeal which had raised millions over the years for young people in this country and abroad but had neglected for years to sort the patched up eye of its mascot Pudsey!

Gary Barlow had never been hotter. His band, Take That had been huge in the 90 s but their re-emergence and sell-out Circus tour had taken them to a new level. They had a big movie hit for the film *Stardust* with *Rule The World*, Gary was being lined up as an *X Factor* judge for the years 2011 to 2013 and Buckingham Palace had come calling.

Ahead, 2012 was to be Her Majesty's Jubilee Year and the Commonwealth Games were to be held in London. The Queen had already asked him to arrange her 86th birthday party. It was a monumental time and he was at the heart of it. Next, she would ask him to deliver a song for the Commonwealth which involved him travelling around the world recording individual lines in multiple countries, resulting in the hit *Sing*. All this was before further sell-out tours solo and with the band plus a venture into musical theatre in *Calendar Girls* and *The Band Musical* which in itself had arisen from his own TV show *Let It Shine*.

To be clear, Gary was red hot. In demand. And working on many projects including charity ones.

This was a massive opportunity right at my fingertips.

But it was also charity and one of the most famous in the country and that meant I had to offer a more than usual display of flexibility. Not only was I working for Gary Barlow but now the BBC and the *Children In Need* team.

The event is to be the second *Children In Need Rocks*, two years on from the first. Gary has personally rung the bands to perform. Radio 1 are covering it with the actor David Tenant, the DJ Chris Moyles and Fearne Cotton at the helm. Jason Donovan is also there.

I am sure that you can appreciate the size of that and the fact that essentially these were three different entities – and a red tape nightmare. It was a PR opportunity and, on occasion, hassle but it was worth it for the collective good of the product and the open road it was taking me down.

Equally, the BBC invested in the event and that meant better production values and budgets. You had to put money in to get money out.

I hope you are keeping up.

Open Road – the debut album for Gary Barlow in 1997.

I know the pressure is on. The coverage of the event means colossal scrutiny and accountability. If there is a fuck up, it is my blame. If it all goes brilliantly, the public gives Gary the credit. That is the deal. I know that he won't see it like that.

Celebs are performing and attending. It is both a cause close to their heart and it is good to be associated with it. Everybody knows the score and everybody is there. I think Biggins even turns up again!

On the night Jamie Cullum arrives. I greet him and he respectfully removes his chewing gum from his mouth.

'Where shall I put it? He asks.

The sense of occasion does at least leave egos at the door.

'In here, ' I reply, holding out the palm of my hand.

He spits it into my hand with a cute grin that melts my heart.

I walk around clutching it for two days.

I persuade a friend of mine to bring a Bentley to auction. Gary agrees to deliver it. £250,000 raised alone in that item. I got the vehicle for nothing and in time went on to secure three in total from my generous benefactor! All the prizes are massive but this is colossal. At auction, we raise half a million alone. The final appeal total exceeds £26 million that year.

It knocks Manchester out of the park.

Black and white dance floor, Perspex chairs, white and silver vases and gifts from *Selfridges* on all the tables. Attention to detail – as ever – king.

Gary was very proud of his northern roots and wanted that reflected in the menu. Starters of mini-burgers, mini fish and chips and mini hot dogs, followed by 500 cottage pies all served in earthenware pots sourced from Holland set the tone. At anything upwards of £500 per head, this was a very serious project.

And I had blagged my way in.

Nothing wrong with that.

Everybody is happy. Job done very well.

It feels like the business has gone to another new level.

Quality of client, plethora of stars; huge sums raised – our own bar too; a lifetime of contacts made for a lifetime ahead...and all for a national broadcaster and a great cause.

I realised this was just another new beginning.

It seemed obvious that we would all work together again.

122

Not before tragedy had struck.

A magnificent winter warehouse wedding.

My moment on 'This Morning'.

When I met my idol, Sharon Osbourne.

Howard Donald wedding.

With Gary Barlow at the Child Bereavement fundraiser.

My co-host at the Child Bereavement fundraister, Gary Neville.

X Factor Wrap Party with Harry Styles.

Kensington Palace, The Winter Whites Ball.

Gary had invited me to the Etihad Stadium as his guest to see the newly reunited Take That perform on The Progress Tour. The band had got back together in 2005 after nine years apart and had exploded back on the scene with their second comeback album which played to sell out stadia and featured almost 250 performers. That was *The Circus*.

Now, they were back again but this was different. For the first time since 1995, four had become five. Robbie Williams was back in the band.

This was *Progress*.

I arrive on my own on a wet night and spot a lone woman in a raincoat, looking a little isolated. In fact, I see her Goyard bag before I clock her.

I had just bought one in New York and nobody else really owned one yet in the UK. I knew that said a lot about her.

Because I knew what it said about me!

However, I had no idea who she was. She was just the girl in the raincoat...with the bag. Just like my Prada clinching the deal in Newcastle, I knew how to start a conversation.

So, I did.

I had just met Ayda Field. Mrs Robbie Williams...and her mother Gwen.

We soon established a mutual level of respect. That world was often surrounded by many sycophants and celebs were normally wise at sniffing them out. We just hit it off. I attended everything thinking there was a potential reason to do so but on this occasion, I wasn't really looking. She just looked alone and I was drawn by her bag.

Moral of the story: I may have been there at Gary Barlow's invitation but you never know who you could be working for next. You can say it was a chance meeting or you can say that it was inevitable.

However, she actually went on to become a friend and her mother a confidante.

She invites me to Milan. Robbie is performing. Would I come along? When I get there Ant and Dec are also there. I am spending the day in the fashion capital of Europe and the boys are there too.

She remains the only woman to have out-shopped me. There is nothing left in Milan by the time we are finished. We are papped with me carrying her shopping bags. On this occasion I will allow myself to play second fiddle.

Our guards are down. We are relaxed, natural. I am actually not looking for work and she is not looking over her shoulder. We are being normal. No agenda.

She invites me to Thanksgiving at hers. Robbie's Mum and Nicole Sherzinger are there as is Adele with her son. Surreal. They are great hosts. But grounded.

I see few excesses of rock 'n' roll and an overdose of normality.

Fans would probably find it dull.

It was an absolute bedrock of stability.

This was a quiet family and friends do. Turkey on the table, early to bed.

As ordinary as rock'n'roll can be!

They ask me to turn their fairytale lifestyle into a winter wonderland and decorate their country home for Christmas.

I suppose that is super stardom though, isn't it? They don't have to work. They have time on their hands. For many, the joy of Christmas is in setting up and making your home feel just that as it comes alive with decorations.

They just ring me!

At the most family-orientated time of the year when people shut up shop for Christmas, I am invited within to create something special knowing that I am trusted personally and respected professionally.

I have become a friend and a person they know can deliver what they want.

I am touched by the relationship because they can obviously say yes or not to anybody and initially Ayda was that lady sat anonymously at the Etihad. We didn't know each other at all. We forged a friendship based on her bag!

This clearly was an easy in for me but our relationship grew into something naturally without there ever being that sense that I wanted to take back from it professionally.

I was always concerned that they might think I had an agenda. Their behaviour to me was totally normal and consistent and never radiated that. It was at the back of my mind only and eradicated largely by the excellent company of Ayda's Mum, who through wise maternal eyes was watching out for her daughter and found me exactly on her level, and small coincidences help. Ayda had her daughter the same year my first granddaughter was born.

We had a lot of opportunity, therefore to form a friendship naturally rather than professionally.

It is not often the case but is extra rewarding when it proves to be so.

It tends to be that you get to know the *famous* in very small doses as you prepare for their event. Their people dominate the conversation. Often afterwards is when the relationship really can blossom and 'their people' disappear.

This *was* different in that I was never going to do a function for Robbie and Ayda. We both just happened to be at a concert on our own.

By the time they asked me to light up their Christmas, it seemed more as a favour than a job.

But clearly as opportunities go, I would *take that* any day.

In 2012, Gary went straight into another round of filming for the *X Factor*.

He was the main man.

Clearly, many people who give their time to charity are moved by personal circumstance. Gary had already been showing his altruistic side for many years but his own circumstances led him further down this path. It's not my business or anyone's but his work in this area resonated even more now than it had done.

By 2013, I was asked to work on another *Children in Need* special – this time in London. It is not quite on the same scale but Gary steals the show yet again.

Barry Manilow also performs. I weigh up his plastic surgery in relation to mine. His wins by a nose.

Gary also concludes his spell as head *X Factor judge* that autumn. Simon Cowell is to return from the USA and Gary has done his stint and has projects queuing up round the block for him.

He asks me to do the show wrap party – the traditional end of series piss-up after the final. Big names in good form – anybody and everybody is there.

I spy Sharon Osbourne across the room.

I don't mind admitting I idolised the woman – probably not too difficult to work out why. We were both Jewish for starters and I reckoned we had each endured some tricky men. But I saw the fighter in her I got when I looked in my own mirror and I recognised what she had done to turn her family into a brand and make that an international sensation. She definitely had the magic touch.

'Let me introduce myself,' I began.

There was nothing to lose.

'You're from the wrong side of the tracks,' I said.

'I'm from the north, you are from the south,' she replied in an instant.

I smiled. She hugged and engaged in a chicken soup contest. My kind of girl.

She was one of the few people I was in awe of whom I actually wanted to meet outside of a working environment. I wanted to learn how she had created that brand and I wouldn't mind knowing *her* plastic surgeon either.

Then she downed tools and joined Nicole and Harry Styles behind the bar.

Priceless memories.

Anything is achievable.

Of his own accord, Gary had helped me immensely. But it was the next phone call that I was really grateful for.

He had passed my number to Julia Samuel, a close friend of Princess Diana and godmother to Prince George. Please could I organise an event for the Child Bereavement Society at Banqueting House, London. It was to be their 21st anniversary dinner. Over 250 people would attend. Gary was to perform and Prince William would speak.

Importantly to me, beyond the sense of occasion, I was now a grandmother and seeing things through slightly different eyes. Plus – I really liked the charity a lot.

On the night Prince William spoke movingly about his late mother. She had attended the charity's launch and had recognised early the need for support for grieving children before her own tragedy struck her boys. Now, William was a father and of course a victim and had taken on that role with the organisation. Equally humbling, Gary and Dawn were committed. Gary would too become a patron. He said on the night that it had always been too painful to talk about their loss – in performance he could find a way to pay 'joyous tribute' and give thanks to the organisation which had helped everyone in the room including themselves.

At its heart, was a massive heart. The cause and the connections would stay with me forever.

My 50th. Dianne's farm. Before we had split. Friends and clients invited.

How the hell do you put on a party for yourself and your friends who have lived on the periphery of your reputation for doing this, and what are you supposed to do when people who have paid you to do the same over the years are also coming?

It is the ultimate test on so many levels.

Firstly, you are no longer dealing with someone else's budget. That dream which you sell them with all those glossy extras suddenly needs refining. You are now your own client.

Then they probably expect you to pull the rabbit out of a hat for your own bash. Surely, this will be the party to top all parties?

Finally, you just have to walk that taste line. You don't want to deliver something that leaves them wondering why you didn't do the same for them, nor do you wish to display such opulence that they probably conclude that at some point they have paid for it.

As you have seen, the very nature of the beast is that clients become friends and friends become clients. The lines are blurred so it wasn't really a case that I could draw a line and not invite clients.

In addition to all this you are only as good as your next party and your party is your reputation – everybody tells someone about a party they went to at the weekend and so your reputation grows and expands. So, my own party remains an advert for my business. My birthday is work.

That's why by midweek in the run up to that weekend, I pulled out!

I told Dianne she would have to take it from here. I didn't want to know! Apart from the potential non-payer the weekend Princess Diana died, I have never done that. It literally was my party and I would cry if I wanted to do.

I approached it with no sense of excitement or anticipation. I would have to smile my way through it. Clearly, when you do something fun for a living, what are you supposed to do for fun?!

I started with good intentions. Up went the marque with mezzanine floor. We would line that with a dessert station. What next? I had been to New York for a party and discovered a brilliant violinist and knew that was an essential booking. Then I discovered this old baby grand piano in amongst some antiques, and painted it red. The violinist had a home for the night – on top of it. I went full on to create that NY city nightclub look. Finally I persuaded the brand *Yo Sushi* to hire out their food belt so we could serve in style all night long. This was the first event that they had allowed the belt to be used.

That's where I drew a blank and told Dianne to step in.

She knew the rules – surprise me but no surprises please! I know, a tough one.

For the first time in all my years in the business, I had a genuine insight into how my clients feel. Each judgement on a daily basis had a cost implication, and I can tell you, those sums only ever went in one direction.

Now, I could afford to throw the party to end all parties if I wanted to but I am sure you appreciate the colossal difference between spending somebody else's money and your own. I now had a completely different perception of budget – and everybody has a different level of what they perceive as value for that money. In short, I wanted a £250,000 party for £20,000!

By the time the evening came, Dianne had pulled it off as I knew she would, leaving no stone unturned. Her creativity always had the wow factor. And I enjoyed it in the end. The danger of course, is that organising your own party is a little distracting when you are in the business of managing everybody else's.

So, I had now almost done it all really – parties for friends, royalty, *pop* royalty, famous TV stars, wealthy families from Jewish to Indian, football, and major corporate players.

That only left one gap.

My own daughters.

Goldie wanted a marquee at Tatton Park.

She was very grungy and bohemian at the time. I don't know what possessed her in the genes to strike out and be so different! Where ever could that have come from? She wanted a baroque feel but also a traditional ceremony and a white virginal wedding so I had to go the rabbi and explain to him that I had good news and bad news. The good news was that would be no female vocals during the ceremony as was standard for an orthodox Jewish wedding and the bad was that there would be a gospel choir! I think I was probably the first person ever to book a gospel outfit at Jewish wedding centre. It *was* well into the new millennium. We all had to be flexible.

We only invited just the 350 for this one! Fireworks erupted as she walked down the aisle. My own team were working the event of course. I later found out nobody was volunteering fast to the responsibility for the choreography of the pyrotechnics!

It was the chance to be a hero or a zero. You could claim this moment for yourself and dine out on it at the office for eternity, or you could risk a disaster with me looking at you strange for the rest of your employment!

Which might not have long left.

Once again, I was the client *and* the organiser but this time, the stress is mounting. Two weeks beforehand, my dress arrives. It doesn't fit and I can't get into it. I have nothing to wear to my daughter's wedding.

I did push the boat out.

I knew I was not getting a quarter of a million's worth of party for 20 grand. That meant flying to Amsterdam and sourcing 350 Moroccan cups and saucers to fit the theme while copper lamps burned.

As befits a traditional Jewish ceremony, it concludes with the groom placing his foot on a glass to symbolise freedom and the finality of the marriage covenant. On its smashing and to the split second, the dividing wall drops and the band strikes up and the trollies are out.

And then we are off.

I am under the canopy, devoid of responsibility for the stage management!

For once.

I never asked back in the office but there appeared to be no error. Heads would not roll.

I was able to be a mother without succumbing to the personal pressure of being event organiser. Only when it got this personal had I ever felt that level of stress.

By the time Katie got married, I made an error of judgement having Roger attend. Things were not good at all. I just didn't realise *how* bad. That complicated matters massively. I felt genuinely sorry for my little girl that I seemed so distracted and distant.

To add to the complexities, the groom's parents were divorced so we were now four parents to deal with!

Katie wanted to be much more involved than Goldie and yet, despite life taking over behind the scenes, I knew I had to run this show. I concluded that if I push her enough, by the end I would get control! Plus – she was based in New York so that in itself presented a challenge.

We had settled on Victoria Warehouse in Manchester as the venue. This was to be the first time it had hosted a wedding. Right up my street. I love that challenge.

In my mind though, that was not the issue to overcome. I had to put this wedding on a par with Goldie's. Unlike almost every other occasion when a family had booked *me* more than once, this was *my* family and I couldn't be looking to better it.

Live on stage, my daughter's guilty pleasure. The Gypsy Kings. Another triumph.

Then, a decade on from my 50th came my…60th. I am glad you are following!

I really did not want to endure the same stress to the point that it consumed me. As you might have interpreted, life was in a very different place.

I only invited 80 people. The venue this time was Gary Barlow's old home, Delamere Manor. My guests included Kenny and Marina Dalglish, the former footballer and pundit Alan

Hansen and his wife Jan plus actress and comedienne Sally Lindsay – another through the Corrie stable.

This time, I had a *lot* of fun preparing my own party placing names on hairbrushes and individual table numbers on hair mouse! I had learned the lessons from before. People had also come to expect the little touches.

But, I was miserable and I think people knew it. The party was the usual success. I deemed it a disaster. That is because of what was going in my head.

There was an elephant in the room.

And everybody knew and had known longer than me.

That elephant did not deserve a place.

It was time to let him go.

My world had fallen apart the night before my Mum's 80th birthday.

October 11, 2012.

Timing always deserted me.

I had ridden it out for so long.

Roger was a steady, understated individual who had few male friends, lost both his parents within six months of each other and had been married previously to somebody in the Jewish community. Of course, we all knew each other. We had dated for 18 months and then he moved in and we were married.

For life.

After that, I am not sure now what the facts actually are. All I do know is that I clung on and on in a trait that really was uncharacteristic of who the rest of me is. We had certainly lasted longer than the other two and maybe I did carry some sense of tradition and believe in the sanctity of marriage. Perhaps in my head, I had told myself that this time it had to work and anything beyond three was getting a bit silly.

The daft thing is – it was the best of all my relationships. I just don't know how much of it was authentic.

The kids blur the issue in my mind because Roger was very good with them. The girls' education was my responsibility to fund and guide but the three were very close in the absence of their own Dad.

He wound up crying for help from some motel in the middle of had.

Furthermore, Roger was very supportive of my business. Remember, I never forgot his advice about going 50:50 with Dianne. I just didn't take it. In the moment, I absolutely felt this support. Now, I can see it afforded him plenty of opportunity which I blindly never stood in the way of. He bought a flat in Spain so he could have his independence and go and play golf. I just didn't realise that he was literally chasing after birdies.

And success did come quickly in that new era with Dianne. I didn't see any jealousy in him and thought he was comfortable in his own skin but I reflect now that he probably did get quite pissed off being invited to everything in that soulless, nameless way of being the 'and guest' on my invite.

I thought this was what marriage was meant to be.

Realistically, at this point in my life, I couldn't have been floating more. Though, I would never accept financial security as ever complete, we were sorted and work was booming; the kids were stable and the pair of us had a good life. Getting ready for Mum's birthday celebrations though was unwittingly the moment I discovered that he actually had a double life.

This, of all nights, too. One of those rare parties I am preparing for *me*, for *my* family, *for* once. No enchanted gardens, and no rock status about – just a small marquee in the garden and 50 of my Mum's closest friends!

One innocent act was all it took to discover the lack of innocence that I had been sharing my life with.

I opened the iPad to book some tickets – just a mundane task in a rare moment of downtime. Roger had been out that night at a corporate do.

There it was.

'Speak tomorrow xxx,' flashed up.

He hadn't been smart enough to delete his history – something in time which would consign him to just that.

Of course, you can look back and say that if I hadn't picked up the tablet on that night then I wouldn't have ever known or you can say that thank goodness I did and I would have found out sooner or later.

When he walked in, I said nothing but sensed he was agitated. Now, whether this angst was caused by me being on the device I do not know or it is possible that I had both had my head stuck up my own arse for so long *and* the fact that I trusted him, feeling settled and *for life* that it was only now that I noticed his behaviour was different.

Your mind over-analyses. You start to see scenes on repeat from the past. You wonder if you have been blind to other moments where he has looked physically like this – the

143

seen a ghost mentality – and you wonder if you have missed them.

I am devastated and from this moment onwards I can be unaware that it will take me the best part of four years to get over it and it will always leave a scar.

I decide not to act instantly. I need to gather more information. Shaking inside, and having to then endure Mum's party made it almost impossible to don my steel-rimmed business hat persona. Somehow, I would hold off until dawn.

The following morning, he is leaving early for a meeting at a local hotel.

I start looking.

God – as I write this. I ask myself for the first time. *Was* he leaving for an early meeting at a local hotel?

I find a little more. It has to be dealt with now.

I call him and tell him to come home.

'What's this? Who is this?' I take a tone with him that I have never ever assumed.

I am hurt, angry but have to keep a control. I have to listen to the responses and turn my radar on.

'It's a client,' he confesses.

'I want her out of the practise.'

I have no other words at this point.

The lies begin.

He is on damage limitation.

Then the bombshell.

'I am addicted to porn,' he goes all Michael Douglas on me as if I am to have sympathy for some sort illness or addiction in this department.

'Porn and this – it's totally irrelevant,' I slam back.

Now, I realise each answer bought him a little time.

'A lot of men watch porn,' I went cold on him. 'It doesn't phase me.'

I dug him in to a corner where he couldn't play that card again because it wasn't going to hurt me. He needed to come up with something better, and of course, now as pathological liars do, when he gave me a tiny drop I was clued up enough even in this state to know that in fact a deluge was waiting to pour.

144

Yet, somehow I was in survival mode too.

I am sure that this moment in my story provokes certain responses from 'we've all been there, love' to 'why the fuck didn't you just tell him to go?' and then obviously, here is my vulnerability laid bare. The hard-nosed bitch who cuts those big deals had found the biggest deal of them all and it was about to derail her. I am sure some would take great satisfaction in the dismantling of my soul but others would find it totally out of character that I might stay and fight.

When I left my first husband with the dinner and dog note, that was essentially who I am. But this is also who I am, finally craving that stability that goes right back to Dad.

I do have a heart and it had just been broken.

Of course, every time you add a little to the lie, it snowballs into an avalanche. She was not just a client. She had been since the April.

I only discover this after a Christmas trip to Oman when something just didn't sit right. I had thrown myself back into work and accepted his lame excuses and had given him the benefit of the doubt.

I know, I know…

'Nothing more than a flirtation,' he protested.

They *had* been flirting but there are some much better verbs when you get into this territory and you realise that the traits you are dealing with are those of a repeat offender.

He had been *cultivating* her.

What does that tell you? The power of the chase, a sexual appetite that would never be fulfilled r match that appetite, the inability to stop, the psychological control and manipulation, the secrecy…need I go on?

She was just the precipice.

The real deal was waiting to explode.

She was an employee…a young clerk and single girl from Ashton-Under-Lyne, just a few miles out of Manchester. She had nothing to lose. If some old bloke wants to pay, spoil you and groom you then you might well say yes.

I have a little more information by the festivities, as you can see. In fact, I make it my mission to find out everything about her. That initial shock and disgust had somehow turned to anger and focus. I was still in the relationship after all and giving it just about everything but you see things differently and keep a little back. You place a preservation order on yourself. You are not quite full on, but generally I was going through the motions of believing in my marriage.

When I returned in the New Year, that bugging-me feeling took hold and it was then – admittedly and naively in delay – when it all unravelled.

I learned her birthday.

I discovered their meetings every Monday morning and Friday afternoon. Then there was the cash machine withdrawal ...to buy *her* a Mulberry handbag.

He had never bought me anything. Ever.

On 1 February, I went undercover! I logged on to Moonpig – something I would almost never do. If only I had. Sooner.

Oh...

Seven cards in as many days.

Explicit.

Now, it began to unravel.

The detail, as anyone in this position will tell you, is almost secondary to the placement of that detail in your own timeline, leaving you one conclusion – that everything had all been a lie.

You had no authenticity.

When you look back at times that you know were happy *at the time* they are sour in the memory because they are fake.

So, in 2012, Eamonn Holmes very kindly agreed to come down and host a *This Is Your Life* for Roger. He was a huge Sheffield Wednesday fan and we managed to include some ex-players from all around the world. When you do this stuff for a living, it is not a fait accompli that you do it your personal life as you have seen but I always wanted to go the extra mile for Roger. Imagine doing what I do and then people who love you (rather than pay you) thinking you can put on a show for everyone else but can't be bothered for them. No, I didn't work like that.

So, I pulled out all the stops.

And he beamed. It was a great great night. A happy memory.

I just didn't know at the time about the mistress 32 years younger than his daughter.

Then, of course, I dug some more.

The more I shovelled, the greater the dirt.

You will not be surprised to learn that I was almost the last to know.

147

Equally, it probably will not shock you that I blamed myself — for almost the first time in my life. I was a good wife but of course, I always put my children and business first. It doesn't really matter and I only understand now that when you are dealing with a sociopath, you could live like a Saint and they will conjure their deceit and part of that process is of course transference where you are the only one walking away with the guilt — so they still win by messing with your head after they have been kicked out of your life.

For me, it was time to re-visit therapy which, on and off, had been part of my life since about the age of seventeen following my parents' split.

At this stage, stupidly, I was still not quitting the marriage. I don't know why now. Me more than anybody was the impulse queen. But I stayed.

Marriage guidance was the next step but really when you need to stoop that low, you are probably doomed. We had counselling together and apart and I am pretty damn sure that he lied from the off in every session.

I just didn't see it at the time. I genuinely believed we were sorting it out and making good progress.

So we chugged along. Yeah, chugged. Of course, work took up so much of my headspace and had to, that I think that whist I was not discovering anything new and his behaviour did not seem out of the ordinary, and we attended the sessions, I guess I wrote it off as a blip. Or that he had reformed.

Stupid, I know.

Only now do I realise that I was throwing away years of my life. What I didn't know was that after every crash point and the subsequent counselling, once the coast was clear, he indulged himself even more.

What was apparent is that I was way behind the ball game and that nobody I knew was really prepared to look me in the eye and speak out. Why do I say this?

Because of the anonymous letter I received in 2015.

It simply was a print out of his match.com profile.

Really, there was no turning back from here. I soon discovered that he was addicted to sites that he shouldn't have been on and talking to people who were generations apart from him.

And yet, I still held on.

I still held on.

By 2013, undercurrents had clearly been rumbling.

I decided to have a facelift. There, if you wanted it, was the perfect opportunity to say I was two-faced.

I didn't do it to save my marriage. I did it to make myself feel good about myself. Which is probably because I did not feel good about my marriage.

Quite likely, this is up there with the top justifications for people in my sort of situation. Though it is true that I felt it was always important to do what you want to feel good and to never rely on anyone else. You can't blame yourself for repeat offenders. That was very much how I had always lived my life.

And I continued to over-dress for work. My staff knew that they should always appear as if Prince Charles was going to walk in or they were going to sell a half a million pound party.

Of course, it is very easy to say that my life was my business and my business was my life and that I seemed a stubborn selfish person but that was only that exterior. Within a marriage, I kept on going with work for Roger and the girls. I did it for him, and yes, he of course said that I actually did it for me.

I understand now that we all need to show vulnerability and that I mothered him and in the process, let him control me. But yes, I bared my soul to Roger. Then, I tore it apart in self-analysis. I knew that I ticked a lot of boxes for him but equally you don't go into a marriage with a shopping list of what applies do you? You evolve into the relationship.

You ask yourself when did it change and then you beat yourself up. I know that I was definitely fun for the first five or six years of the relationship which amounts to only a quarter of our time together but what happened next and at what point? When did the fun go for him? Or could he just not help himself? Is it character defined rather than personality clash, boredom or circumstance? Today I know it is the former.

What happened was ripping me right apart and leaving me emotionally shattered by the deceit. Not having the last word on the outcome was new territory too.

Today, I reflect that actually he made me realise that I am successful and worthy and much of what happened is the reason I continue to grow when it would have been easier to roll over and die.

Sometimes, it takes a stranger to wander into your life to help you get context. In many ways they can be more comfortable calling it when they don't know the whole story nor the ins and outs of your *life* story...

I had been recommended to organise a charity event for one of the world's ultimate networkers. If ever there was anyone so full of shit but so adorable too in his insecure way, it was this person.

'Is that Liz Taylor?' the American accent purred at the end of the phone.

'Yes, but not the one you slept with,' I replied. 'It's the one you've been introduced to.'

The late David Gest was on the line – a man hugely influential in American music, especially amongst The Jacksons – but essentially a complicated charismatic individual with a bag of problems himself, yet in whose company you would always want to be.

Of course, I had heard the Liz Taylor stuff so many times. To everyone new cracking that comedy opener, they assume that a guest slot on *Mock The Week* will follow.

For me, well...you can either tire of it or play it to your advantage.

I would regularly call a restaurant (even today) and say 'It's Liz Taylor speaking, please can I get a table for 1230'.

Even though most people do know that she has passed away, it still invokes a knee jerk reaction.

I am rarely turned down.

It certainly gets you through the awkwardness of the opening gambits of a conversation.

It has followed me since I was old enough to understand who she was. The truth is that I was named after my maternal

151

grandmother. My brother Robert got off lightly which I always considered both standard and unfair!

I won't go as far as to say that Dad was controlling me and casting shadow by cursing me with a name like that from birth because all I did was play on it. I never asked him if he thought it was funny.

Even Prince Charles played the Liz Taylor card:

'You are the *other* Liz Taylor,' he greeted me.

'No, I am *the* Liz Taylor,' I replied.

I was never intimidated by royalty. When you line up waiting for your five seconds and everyone is on pins trying to say the right thing, it never bothered me. Tell it like it is.

I arrived in Turkey once to deliver a function for long-standing clients. As I came through Arrivals at Istanbul Airport, the usual card for the waiting car was being held aloft for me.

Suddenly, I walk into the flash and glare of TV lights and cameras, hastily retreating to recording the arrival of the Hollywood star.

Even though she died in 2011.

Some years later, it seems the news had not yet arrived in Turkey.

And now David Gest was at it too. But, he is forgiven and he could not have wandered into my life at a better time. Better – in that he brought all his eccentricity to my world and my God now was the time for that.

Not better – in that my life had become challenging.

'What the fuck are you doing with this guy?' he asked me over lunch.

He had all the answers to everyone's problems except his own. Didn't we all. I loved his craziness and he was very easy to get to know fast without, of course, ever getting to know him at all. In short, the maddest guy on the planet was giving me the best advice.

'Don't let a man treat you like that,' he would say.

As a man.

It started to resonate.

But, I still hung on.

We are in Hong Kong the following February. I am organising a party for someone whom I have known since the age of eleven. I am – I understand now – going through the motions. And through the emotions. At the time, I am showing intent. I am still believing what I am being told despite the years of lies which you can see clearly here. I still hold out for reconciliation.

You can tell things are not fine at all. The conversation is poor.

I tell him his new website looks really good.

Maybe I have run out of things to say.

'What do you mean?' he replies foolishly.

The correct answer should have been 'thank you'.

Instead, perhaps on guard with the suspicion that I was tracking him, he is standoffish.

'Give me your phone,' I encourage so I can point out the improvements.

In fact his guard was down.

His pants might as well have been too.

Open on the screen a young girl – age unknown but not quite a woman – legs a kimbo.

How do you explain that? In the middle of Hong Kong in the middle of the day in full view of me – once I got his phone, of course. At least save it for his seedy little flat in Altrincham. It tells you everything about the level of addiction, the inability to stop, the disdain for myself and the lifestyle to which he had been so accustomed and the mockery he was therefore making of any counselling.

It was a sham. Everything was a lie. He knew it.

He flew back home unexpectedly.

I had to stay. The party wouldn't organise itself.

The show must go on.

Again.

Later that year at Christmas, David has been dead since the April, found in his hotel room in Canary Wharf where he seemed to be living, I am in Tenerife with my family.

The TV show *Millionaire Party Planner* is on. We have had no preview tapes. It is a show about me and my business.

153

It was the nail in our coffin.

I know that I have lost him. It is though that he cannot bear to watch. Does he hate me? Is it jealousy? Do I seem fake to him? Or has the penny dropped that in his eyes, we are so far apart, even though mine I hadn't seen it?

I wasn't necessarily seeking approval or wanting him to be proud of me. That's bullshit, isn't it? I know that I shouldn't have even cared by this point but I cannot explain why I still did other than craving a structured home life for once. Business was always mad. You wanted to retreat every night after everything back to something normal. In truth, he hid behind the chaos and it allowed him to play in public.

And as I was about to find out, my goodness…was he playing.

How do you carry on working? Work gives you focus. Your team bale you out in a way you only realise retrospectively. You slack on the time-keeping, proceed on auto-pilot during the day and become on first name terms with every barman in your neighbourhood.

The phone still rings. You still perform.

But you are largely in the business of delivering for those people who are at the peak of their success and happiness when you can only share one of those sentiments, however much in denial you are.

The show had to go on.

The intensity of the work helped in the short term – I would resort to type and live in character, steely-eyed and with razor sharp focus the tougher the deadlines and demands got. But I was playing the character of me.

In the long term, I was supressing emotion that was just being stored up waiting to explode, taking me right to the edge of a nervous breakdown. The requirements of the job brought a double edged sword. The need to take yourself off around the country and the world and produce functions in the evening meant that I was delaying much-needed time to stop and think but was also still in the zone for my business. So, in denial, that meant I couldn't know fully what he was up to and I could destroy myself second-guessing or I could continue to take at face value all the lines he trotted out which were putting severe distance between his mouth and the truth.

So when I got the call to go to Bury St Edmunds in Suffolk, the voice at the end of the line found me in ruthless mode. It was also a classic me opportunity.

'Our wedding planner has let us down,' he said. 'It's a disaster.'

The groom to be was Mark Wright, star of the reality show *The Only Way Is Essex*. He was due to marry the actress

Michelle Keegan who was already known to me through her role as Tina McIntrye in *Coronation Street*.

I had three months to save the day.

I like a challenge and boy did I need it at this point.

Initially, Mark was *that* challenge, him calling me one morning hungover following an awards ceremony the night before.

He was now ringing to say could we reschedule the meet planned for later that day. I had just driven four hours to Hengrave Hall.

'No,' I replied. 'If you do not get your arse moving in the next 60 minutes, I am not doing it.'

Then I hung up.

This was who I was but possibly too, who I was becoming in light of my impending darkness.

Mark duly turned up slightly ragged, still feeling the effects of the night before.

I was in no mood to mess – but I would have said the same to anyone at any stage of my life. Simple rules: I always make you feel like you are my only client. You are never my only client! You hired me. Get to work.

He got the message.

'This is my wedding planner,' Mark announced in his speech. 'Don't mess with her.'

I didn't mind at that point.

I had already pulled the marquee down and moved the location on the day. They didn't dare argue.

He could see I had pulled it off. Though of course by the time the toasts are being done and their relief is kicking in at the warmest of welcomes they received through streets lined with well-wishers and the 20 trees and dozens of flowers at the ends of the aisles in the grounds of St. Mary's church and the Tudor mansion Hengrave Hall, you are only halfway through your day. But that first section is where all eyes are watching and detail is king. After that, I can breathe out a little before taking another deep one in for the rest of the night.

For Mark and Michelle that is the moment they start to relax – a million photos done for *Hello!*

156

The world, of course, then gets to see those pictures and sometimes forms a judgement that another showbiz couple sell their soul to the highest bidder without knowing the people or how it works, and most people reading this would probably jump at the chance to do the same.

There is an inevitability too that two people in love get dubbed 'showbiz couple' and 'it will never last' and is somehow plastic. The truth is that here was a fantastic northern girl with modern values and a bloke whom TV had made famous but was just a normal guy – neither of whom bore much resemblance to characters they played on TV even if they were playing themselves, nor the way they had been traditionally written up in the press.

Mark is not flashy. TV shows you the persona and not the person. As I was soon to find out myself.

They were being dubbed the new 'Posh and Becks' which was ridiculous and something they would have only laughed at. Their families were close tight-knit communities. The chef from their favourite restaurant in Essex did the barbeque on the night. Mark and Michelle got the evening going with a brilliantly choreographed and highly emotional interpretation of that dance in the movie *Dirty Dancing*. His best friends had also rehearsed a cameo. Here was a guy *just* marrying the girl he loves. They were who they were and not what they or someone else wanted them to be.

It left me slightly in awe.

'Blimey, the room didn't look like this last night.'

I had found myself organising a function as another was clearing up. We had the venue for the second of two nights.

I had half a day to build three stages and line the room with red fabric.

Anyone who had been at the previous evening's entertainment would be blown away by our attention to detail on both the little things and the big ones.

You would be left wondering how the same venue could put on two evenings so different, and in such a short space of time.

The room didn't look anything like it had the previous night.

It was Neville Neville who commented.

Neville was the late father of the former Manchester United footballers, Phil and Gary. Through my long association with the club and by the nature of the fact that Gary was a one club man, I had known the family for a very long term. Gary had probably been to almost every party I had thrown for them from the mid-nineties once he had broken into the first team.

Time can build respect. It affords you the opportunity to show integrity. When a player comes out of the sport, their world changes overnight and even though many are now wealthy, there is still a lot of life ahead and circles can change. You look to what you know and to whom you can trust. It helps that I knew Gary's father well and that both of our sardonic sense of humours connected. You need to speak the language of these people. That is an absolute essential.

Gary first came to see me when he was getting engaged. Once more, it was the Swan Band that was the carrot. Time and time again, my instinct towards my Parisien friends had been correct. Every party had a memorable element but if you left with no outstanding memory, you would always remember the band. He had seen them many times, doing frequently changing sets. He knew they were a class act and a must for his wedding when frankly he probably could have booked most rock stars on the planet.

Often we speak about nothing in particular – just sounding each other out. A lot of people want to know Gary through his many roles. You have to cut down the number of people you really take counsel from. One thing that I have learned over the years is that to buy into the person, you have to do the same to the people around them. I know that Robbie and Ayda Williams trusted me partly because I spent so much time with Ayda's Mum who was of similar age to me and not in their spotlight. If she said I was OK, then I probably was.

It had happened to me many times before I realised that it was a smart way to gain insight into the people you were trying to do business with. Somebody always had their ear. The chef Tom Kerridge's wife was another. I learned a lot about Tom through Beth.

With Gary, I became quite close to his wife Emma after organising their wedding. It is probably safe to say that he is one of the individuals who has opened more doors for me than most. Apart from his continuing connections with the football club and his very high profile work for Sky Sports, he has his fingers in a lot of pies in Manchester. There isn't a person he can't connect to and barely a building he hasn't built. Well, not quite but it seems that way. When it came to the opening in 2017 of the Manchester celeb hotspot Mahiki which had been closed for ten months, Gary and Ryan Giggs put their money in as he had done many times before. It was a rare occasion when someone placed *me* on their VIP guest list...just behind his good mate David Beckham!

He is Mr Manchester. I stress that point not to name drop but to emphasise his huge sphere of influence.

And with all that going on, he can bulldoze into a meeting but it is Emma you listen to. I got that when they came to me for their wedding. She seemed shy under her knitted hat. Perhaps, they had both learned that it was wise to keep their guard up when they probably have to deal with a lot of bullshit. But I could see instantly once the masks were down that she was the force behind Gary. You don't get to organise someone's big day without getting to know them. A wedding is meant to be the summit of a girl's dreams. Obviously I have been to that summit three times *but* to understand that person's wishes you have to understand that person's life. That is how we formed the connection.

On the back of that hundreds of other connections have evolved. Emma is now a child bereavement councillor. Together for that charity and Red Sea Pedestrians, (an organisation of North West businessmen and women who raise money for various groups), we have all joined forces on several occasions with Gary Barlow and Kym Marsh from Corrie who has also suffered child loss, to fundraise further and increase awareness.

I know I am good at connecting people. Charity can often be that glue. Gary and Emma and Gary and Dawn are great examples of how the conversation has moved over the years and yet there is a constant to it all.

An enquiry into booking my band because you saw them the day your team won the F.A. Cup ends up with that person's own wife training to help families who had suffered the death of a child and then fundraising for that organisation of her own accord and becoming friends was an incredibly beautiful conclusion to what, after all, started as a piece of business.

It doesn't get much better than that.

And the story won't end there…

I couldn't think of a worse time in my life to appear in my own reality TV show. So, I did.

Channel Four had come calling and recognising the huge expansion in the party industry, asked me if I would star in a fly on the wall documentary.

The truth is that my PR guru and lifelong friend, Sarah Lewis and myself had been casually pushing for an opportunity like this for some time.

We weren't actively pursuing it but we had had conversations about *me* the brand. Fly on the walls had been a mainstay of British television for a couple of decades. They had covered everything from driving lessons to a hotel kitchen. It was definitely on our radar at the right moment and opportunity.

I thought I had nothing to lose. As you know, I wasn't thinking straight at all around this time. I kept Roger off screen – much to his annoyance as I had since found out and the only airtime they would get of me would me acting the part of me in the role.

I had twice previously been asked to contribute to similar shows for a programme called *That's Rich* and another called *Working Girls* and had over the years clocked up many TV appearances. But this was now different. I was the focus. Party planning was in vogue.

In *That's Rich,* there was the softer side of me but an incomplete picture. I was pitched as the wedding planner. In *Working Girls* – a show which also featured the likers of boxer Ricky Hatton – I was able to mentor young girls who didn't really have a sense of work per se and seemed oblivious to the possible rewards of the lifestyle achievable through hard work, whatever that industry they chose was. I showed them the personal values that they could achieve through graft. The *show* showed me as a mentor, able to connect with young people.

Bar the odd TV appearance as a pundit – such as the millennium when of course it was time to party like it was 1999 –

these were longer opportunities showing sides of my character that you might not see working with me or hiring our services. *Working Girls* – I would realise in time – served me well and enabled me to move towards areas of education and 'lecturing' young people which would give me enormous personal reward. It was hard work but very interactive. I had a taste that I might want to do more.

Of course, when you have finished filming, you start working with Sarah and thinking where this can go. We both knew that post Dianne, I had evolved into a real personality-led business. It was obvious really that someone with such a forceful personality as me might set themselves free if I was the whole of something rather than half of it. So that is where the *me* brand really began to evolve even though I had obviously my own stamp on what I do since day one. You start to build that individual brand out of the brand – and then the phone doesn't ring!

So when Endemol Shine did call to make this show for Channel 4, it was a little out of the blue.

That meant for six months of my life – close to the most disastrous time personally I have ever lived for, not only am I performing for potential customers but I am doing the same for the cameras as well.

I was wary – there had been some horrendous programmes in this field. I was happy – in that they only asked me. On some days, I would convince myself it was a free advert for the business; on others I would just tell myself to get through and pray to survive the edit.

I was *very* lucky that some of my friends and long-standing clients like Marina Dalglish were happy to allow the cameras to film – for Marina it was simply good publicity for her charity. They might have a pop at me in the editorial but you could only show a woman raising money for such good causes in a favourable light.

Marina and Kenny had always been brilliant so it was unsurprising. I count them both as dear friends even though I can rarely understand Kenny to this day – he speaks so fast and is still so Scottish after all his years on Merseyside that sometimes

I have to re-ask the question to Marina to make sure I have got the gist of what he has said. The beauty too is that like all wonderful friendships, they were just two people to me. I had never seen Kenny as an icon. That is because I didn't get football!

I think Kenny enjoyed Marina's centre stage though – for once it put him in a corner where the spotlight didn't shine. Of course, I understand that the Dalglish surname resonates with influence across so many sectors of British society. He is an icon and of course, knowing them means one thing leads to another.

From her initial request to book the Swan Band, the relationship had just grown. I was then able to ask one of my clients to sponsor the band for her breast cancer charity and then before we know it, I am organising her children's weddings and in her relentless pursuit of fundraising, we had nearly clocked up a decade worth of work together. From there, I was introduced to Liverpool Football Club itself and naturally that leads me to Steven Gerrard in his boxers and everything else that has followed.

The simple rule of thumb remains – everybody at a party is going to have a party themselves.

I was grateful that they agreed to appear – I needed that credibility on screen. I would not have lived up to my billing if I could only deliver bar mitzvahs.

Many of my famous or big corporate clients didn't want to know. If the show wanted to see inside a millionaire's home, then that was not going to happen.

You don't get to see the final edit of course before it airs. The night before it was shown, I was petrified.

We were on what was to be our last family holiday in Tenerife. It was 30 December 2015.

And they did have a little pop. Some of the edits seemed elongated – for example, if a client paused in responding to a suggestion. Naturally, they cut in moments of dialogue where I might suggest a theme only for it to be rejected. The tone of the voiceover could always telegraph to the viewer what they were meant to think.

'My first impression is its shite,' is my opening line.

They are the first things you hear me say but the opening shot is of me squealing as one of my suppliers shows me the half-dressed mannequin sat on my specially installed bar. Half-dressed isn't even half of it. The doll is covered in fresh flowers.

Then they cut to me in a restaurant looking awkward eating my food and before the opening theme rolls I am on camera saying 'Fuck it, I'm expensive but you get an amazing product.'

It leaves you in no doubt as the type of person they want the viewer to see – and I accept that to a degree some of it is me.

'Eamonn Holmes, you'll have to wait,' I bark as the phone rings while I am on another line.

That is just for the cameras. I always take Eammon's call.

It's high energy – at times it looks like chaos. I am name-dropping by the end of the first minute, which of course is far too late for me and I look a right luvvie when I intro myself with 'The secret to a party is…moi'.

I hated it. Detested it. Loathed and despised it. I never wanted to see it again.

I have, of course since watched it back and have relented a little. It is very hard as the subject of a show like that to evaluate if it is real and accurate and part of that emotion is because you are aware of how much you filmed. You start to say things like 'why did they pick that bit' or 'that's not quite what happened' or 'they have made that look worse from that angle' or 'there was another line in there before I gave that look and answer'.

Surely, those people who know me or who have worked with me watch and draw the line about halfway through. You do question how your clients will view you now.

I am sure Eamonn and Ruth would be laughing and saying 'Well, she is a little like that…'

And I am.

But this is a performance in a performance industry and I am both playing up for the cameras and playing me while the real *me* is struggling on every front.

I am pleased about one element in the opening sequence even though the footage and narrative is a little cliché. They begin by showing images of what a party used to look like – a couple of bits of cheese on a cocktail stick and a little bit of *Babycham* and a sense of awkward Britishness on show.

That helps me as they cut to aerial shots of big Cheshire houses each with a pool and start branding about the huge sums people will pay for parties. It is a good line because it affirms the point that if you have money and you want to do it properly, then there are professionals like me who can and will but also once upon a time this did not exist at all. I feel good that certainly in the North West, I am one of the few who both remembers that non-existent era and built something out of it.

Then you self analyse your look and immediately change your hair colour whilst speed-dialling your plastic surgeon. You ask why they *didn't* include certain bits and if they were actually filming things you thought they were and vice-versa while you thought you were off camera.

You forget one simple fact when you watch it back. The public only see the final one hour show. They do not see the process. And for Channel 4, they watched in their droves. TV ratings are not what they were – few Channel 4 shows bar *Big Brother* in its peak have regularly surpassed 4 million viewers. We clocked 1.5 million and more than 1.75 million tweets!

Oh yes – that was the new devil in the detail – everyone was now a critic and every critic had a phone and an opinion.

You scroll for a bit – smile at a few positive comments, shriek back into your soul when someone slaughters you. Then you switch your phone, realising that everybody is watching the same show but nobody seems to be. I take full responsibility for doing it. Many people since have disagreed with me that I had a shocker.

It is an impossible situation to analyse especially when you have to work out what is true and what is fake in your own life.

Of course, unless you are stalking me you probably do not even recall the show.

For a few weeks, I would get stopped. One lady in *Selfridges* in Manchester nudged her daughter and I heard her saying 'that is that woman of that Millionaire Party Planner'.

It was neither good nor bad, just in the end unnecessary.

To my amusement and surprise and when I had mellowed slightly, an invitation popped in the post to attend some national TV awards. I didn't think for one moment we would win and soon I knew before the show had even started!

Waiting in the melee at the drinks reception beforehand with many celebs already well on their way, I was leaning against a radiator when a piece paper tucked behind it fell out.

It was a document containing the show calls for the night and I could see next to our award, it simply read 'Table 7'.

Well, 'that's that,' I thought. We were not on Table 7. We hadn't won.

Walking away and feeling disappointed at being gong-less from a TV show I did not particularly enjoy would have been two-faced anyway really.

I told the team:

'We have not won – we are not on seven. We are going to have sit this out and practise our sincere but disappointed smiles'.

I was too hasty.

The person who was *presenting* the award was on table seven.

The winners were…us.

How funny and what a tonic. People really did have a different perception to the show than myself. I assume, after all, that it wins because of the content in it – in other words us – rather than the huge skill of the production team being lauded! I will take that as a yes.

'Best Business Documentary' apparently!

At the National Reality TV awards.

If the two go hand in hand!

'Why not make a series?' people were now asking.

I will pass thank you.

There was a danger too that you might not get out alive if you went down that route – and it could have an adverse effect on the day to day running of the business. Six months for one show was acceptable. A longer period of time might be disruptive and you couldn't know from one client to the next if

166

they would welcome the intrusion. The project would remain a one-off.

Last word and a little snapshot of what the industry can be like goes to the entertainer Bobby Davro, whom I had met several times previously.

Unless I am very much mistaken, he completely blanked me before the ceremony. Afterwards, he virtually clambered over the tables to congratulate me.

That's showbiz.

The truth was that my own life had now become a drama itself.

The phone does not stop ringing after *Millionaire Party Planner*. I have to take that as the only benchmark that counts. Never mind an award. Let's face it. If five people called and booked me on the back of it but one million people hated it, that is still a decent piece of business because those five people will invite their world into my world and from that other parties will grow.

I don't think those are the numbers by the way but you see the point. The show underlined to me that you have to understand your unique selling point. If you don't get niche, you won't get work. People who hire me are a certain type of person or business. Whilst I will talk to everybody, not everyone will hire me.

I am only aiming at a certain end of the market.

The top end.

I give my team a clear remit of what I will do. We do continue to talk to production companies all the time. You never know when you will be needed or your genre will be in vogue for a moment or a sustained period of time. All it takes is a royal wedding, a Trump visit and state banquet, a footballer's wedding, a new year…all the usual ingredients and suddenly TV wants you.

Significantly, whilst that industry was as fickle as mine and phases would come and go, one thing that the show did do for me was launch me in to public speaking. So, the roots in mentoring were in *Working Girls* but now anybody from corporates to universities were calling to see if I could go to do talks.

It took me some time to realise that this was the success of the show that I could actually measure. The night it aired, I am scrolling down the *Daily Mail* comments taking it so personally when everyone calls me a bitch, failing to understand at the time that many who commented had not even seen the programme. I am also vulnerable because I am abroad and there is no support from Roger.

In effect there is no Roger.

If there is an opposite of the icing on the cake analogy then this is it. My marriage is down the pan, I am getting slaughtered online and now my husband, in name alone, essentially disowns me and the broadcast and the two go hand in hand together.

In time – and that really did hurt – I realise that this is a minority. The award – in the Business Category – should have been a clue that it was more credible than I had suspected. But for twelve months after it aired, I was forging this new career as a speaker and that was the evidence that it had been a hit.

People were interested – in me, the business side of the business, the stories, the showbiz, the money, the detail. All of it – and it brought a different aspect when we would get the call sounding out my availability. Students wanted to know about fashion and starting out, everyone wanted funny stories and of course, the numbers people would spend blew everyone away. I was also an entrepreneur and particularly amongst the young, seen as aspirational not for turning up in a Porsche with a new designer handbag after a facelift but because I had started something which didn't exist and it turned into a million pound plus brand – and that start up mentality resonated with the teenagers of the digital generation as much as the trappings which could follow.

It is safe too that I often got asked a lot about Michelle and Mark's wedding. For whatever reason that too represented a re-birth and re-positioning of me. If it were a university module you would look at it and conclude it had all the elements – not least because it represented the fusion of an actress from the most successful British TV show ever and a personality from the new era – reality TV. That made it mass appeal to every generation. People were nosey and they wanted the detail.

From this, I took confidence which had been shattered by the TV show in the moment and *in the moment* I was living too. I later learned that the programme had aired in many other countries too. TV people clearly viewed it as a success.

So, even though I hated the show and my life was falling apart, I did begin to listen. Other people like Sarah were telling me I had got it wrong – that I was being too sensitive and that it was a platform to build from.

So, it was not just the phone at the office which rang.

I spotted Eamonn's hands at work.

Would I go for a screen test at ITV with a view to hosting a regular slot on whatever it is I do again?

Of course…

And so I arrived at the London studios just as the daily show was finishing, walked on to the set…and made a right pig's ear of the whole thing. I came back grumpily and told Sarah they didn't like me which is daft really because they had had me on before and would have me on again. They liked me enough to audition me.

It just didn't work out but that comment reflects that my head was a in a major wobble. For the first time in my working life, a huge element of self-doubt was more than kicking in. I am not a TV pro but I should have been able to walk that screen test. I became very emotional about the whole experience though as I look back now, I am sure that I was not really tearful about being on telly or not. It was simply the vehicle through which my broken heart was being driven. This was the channel for my emotion, if not my TV career.

I guess the timing was not right for me at that moment. These things happen. That is life.

But this was a golden opportunity, and I blew it.

Why?

My nerves were shot to pieces.

Home had become a disaster. So you go away again abroad to repair. Again.

How many make or break holidays can a couple have?

On the beach in Spain, he tells me he wants to reconcile. This is Spain – Roger's getaway. The truth is he is all at sea and he has all but set sail. These are the words of a pathological liar who knows it has gone but finds himself confused by his own web of lies that the truth is not something he can see any more.

Of course, the effect of a pathological liar on his victim – and I really do not wish to use that word – is that *that* person when dealing with somebody so convincing can be deluded into convincing themselves that *this time*, it *can* work.

Again.

I know that once more, you read this and shout 'how many more chances, Liz?' or 'you, of all people, you are so strong-minded, how can you be so weak?'

The control freak has lost control. The survivor is wilting away.

I know, I know.

Again.

I don't recognise the person I see in the mirror at this point. The mask is down and the only refection I see is the tear-stained four-year-old craving paternal love by demanding piano lessons for her fourth birthday.

That's what this is about.

When the moment finally comes to walk away, I have learned too much.

When we return home from that trip, he says he will fetch his stuff from his flat up the road where he had been living temporarily. This was one of our rental properties into which he moved.

As he comes up the pathway, I see Roger but I see no suitcase.

That's it.

He can't go through with it.

Unbelievable, I know.

You would suspect a character like this would come back for more, go dark for a bit and then with even greater security, re-enter his little world. He always came back. I don't believe that the reason he didn't come back (better than 'left me') was because he had someone better to go to. He must have known what he stood to lose and probably had a sense of how our small cliquey Cheshire society might turn their back on him, but perhaps this time he knew that he could not perpetuate any more lies.

Plus, the truth was unravelling and that very community which I was about to learn had almost hid him, or turned a blind eye to his misdemeanours, were unlikely to shield him any more.

171

And so it proved.

I acquired his phone records.

It was all there – the 2 am phone calls when I had been working away…the Fridays when I had been observing the Sabbath, he had been in bed with a girl…the flat…he was living in that I had assumed had been rented out for years but it turned out to be his little love nest.

Of course, a businesswoman like me should have checked the rent but that fell under home life and not work, so I assumed, didn't I? Never assume. The point about happiness and stability is not looking over your shoulder. I had to do that every single day with work. No wonder, I took it for granted at home.

The more I discovered about what went on, the less I took it seriously. In the moment, it kills you, but only after a considerable period of time do you realise that it isn't you. It's him.

That a cliché but you can do nothing to stand in the way of an addictive personality with sick fantasies on repeat. It took me nearly four years to realise this afterwards but there was still a long way to go to get to that point.

As the saying goes, if it doesn't kill you, it makes you more interesting at parties.

I begin the process of divorcing him. He is gone by the end of September 2016. The paperwork is concluded by the following March.

I send him packing with everything he brought to the relationship – three thousand pounds and two candlesticks.

If he was always counting on some sort of payout I made it clear in no uncertain terms that what I knew was worth more than anything he could counter with. I was wise to how he thought. I hadn't forgotten how he had been banking on a multi-millionaire client of his to leave substantially for him in his will when he passed away. That person ultimately left him nothing. That friend had seen the light sooner than I. By that point, he knew that I *knew* everything and that left him in no position to argue.

This remains the only occasion where I didn't care for a risk assessment on the candle.

Then, it got worse. As the split became public, one by one individuals began to approach me. Every new piece of information that took me forward sent me in the other direction too.

Mentally, it knocked me for six as the latest detail emerged but also, without any particular new information, your mind just flits itself off to conversations, trips (together and apart) words, glances, bank statements and all those marriage counselling sessions which were clearly a sham.

And then there is dissecting the untruths. Which of the partial lies masqueraded a greater fib? That night before Mum's birthday, he bought himself time and responded with the bare minimum. What came out of his mouth had been undoubtedly a lie but what kills you is then second-guessing of what he didn't tell you.

When you accept the answer that it is just a bit of flirting with a client but then later discover it is that and so much more, you dissect every piece of every conversation. This is how people have breakdowns. Were all those 'I love yous' fake? Did even one of them mean anything? All those times I was working and said 'I'll be back tomorrow, I will probably finish up around 3 am here' was he planning that as an opportunity? Yes.

Everything I learned was having a ripple effect. It even made me question my friends, some of whom had been aware without necessarily knowing but I now understand why they had gone a bit quiet in my life. What do you do in this situation as a *friend?* Some stayed quiet to protect me – one in particular said nothing because my own daughter was getting married and the timing plus the sanctity of marriage made it the wrong thing to do at that time.

It was all coming out now. A client of mine, whose daughter had also been getting married, then told me he had slipped his phone number into her handbag at the end of a dinner in our home.

The best one was the apartment in Spain. How stupid had I been? He would tell me every year that he was going out around spring time to open up the flat. Early autumn, he would go back to shut it down.

I thought nothing of it. Now, I find myself saying 'to open up the flat'…and then repeating it out loud followed by a 'for fuck's sake'. He wasn't a cricket groundsman who needed to lock up the pavilion for another six months. It was a flat in Spain. You opened it up by putting the key in the door and walking through the entrance.

It is one of those lines that when you raise it with your friends a couple of years later they can only offer 'well we thought it was an odd thing to say' but clearly not enough proof to come to me with.

Because they didn't know about the prostitutes he was opening it up with.

Or how he was paying for it. The bank account set up in my name in the British Virgin Islands was the answer. Poirot had nothing on me!

And these were not virgins.

So you can probably see, I can get past the sex addiction and the level at which it was manifesting itself but I can't get past the deceit. And obviously, you will be smart enough to work out that I am leaving huge elements of this *out*. Suffice to say, that good old trusty iPad and the ever dependable history section plus those always reliable phone records took me to a place and websites where only the depraved frequent and where there is no ID check on the door.

So in the dark was I, and I think so embarrassed were some people who had clearly known, that when it became common knowledge, it was almost a sense of relief for our friends and acquaintances.

I now understand those close to me did not want to be responsible for something that was not broken *up,* even though it was clearly evident to them to be broken down. There is a difference.

One close friend had stopped speaking to me when I got together with Roger. She was the first person at my door when it all went wrong. We just picked up where we left as true friends do. She had never liked him but had withdrawn to bite her tongue. Sometimes it is easier to do so when you already know what you know and that was before any of us even knew.

To those people on the periphery of our world, I know some people felt that I had got what I had deserved but that really has to be a shallow point of view. Few understood how I lived in my personal world and they might have seen or heard of the tough me at work so you could allow them the thrill of envy if my business had gone bust. And that was the only context in which they thought they knew me.

This was different altogether – my marriage had gone.

But my business sure as hell survived.

35 Jenny In A Bottle

It went from bad to worse.

Fast.

Every new low left you staring into an even deeper abyss.

'I think you should have an HIV test,' one of councillors rang to tell me.

What?

'I think you should have an HIV test,' she repeated.

As I said, just when you thought it couldn't get any lower.

The ultimate punishment for something I hadn't done.

There are two ways of looking at that and I didn't have the strength to ask. Either the counsellor said this every time when there has been infidelity or she had a very strong gut feeling that bordered on knowledge.

Remember – we were having joint sessions and separate ones. I really don't know how many lies he told and if, when alone, he spun the same ones or confided a truth. I am sure that, on his own, he could work his deception with any turn of phrase he wanted to get himself an easier time when we were in there at the same time. That kind of character knows how to manipulate the conversation before it begins.

Then again, he may have turned all needy and equally manipulative with the biggest sob story on the planet. I can't second-guess.

All I know is that I hit the bottle. Hard.

I would go to work, leave the office for once at the same kind of time society deemed normal, and go to the pub. I realise obviously that it was about the worst thing I could do but I do understand that at moments like this people feel it is the way to lift the weight of the world from your shoulders.

It leaves you with a lot of thinking time – some of it straight and clear, the rest wild and confused. You could get past the big stuff like infidelity, the prostitutes, the money...but the incidental detail would kill you and leave you lingering on a thought for ages. I had always wanted to go to India – he had booked it. That irritated me. Of course, I could still go tomorrow if I wanted but that is not the point. It all comes under the heading of sacrifices you make for the greater good when actually nobody else was making any and there wasn't any good in it at all

And for reasons like that, it took me a long time to accept that it was over – not because I loved him but because of the deceit. To this day, people still tell me that he was inappropriate with them.

I was starting to fall apart like I had never done before.

Of course, I still had to put my face on in the morning but turning up for work was getting later and later. I was just not used to dragging myself from a tear-stained pillow every morning.

And that wasn't me at all.

The whole speed and zest for life was gone, paralysed in those moments of solitude and facing a mountain every morning to begin the process of starting again.

When I got to the office – now sometimes even at 11 am, I could still turn it on and delivered some of my finest work during this period. You have to – or I would have no business today. I reminded myself that I needed to work.

I had responsibilities – to my daughters, my mother and my team. I couldn't collapse in front of them. So much of the business was me and they all bought into the standards I set and the personality we led with that if the lights went out, they wouldn't come back on. I couldn't even let them see me dim or flicker yet business suffered with my turnover decreasing and my desire to network weakened. My reactions and speed of thought were slower too.

I just didn't really realise at the time that, whilst I found enough strength for enough hours in the day to lead them, they were without a shadow of a doubt carrying me.

The emotional turmoil is of course compounded by the practicalities of where your life goes now. I knew that as much as I loved my family home, it was time to go.

It was a happy house too but after 29 years, I walked out on it in 2017 and never went back. And I mean never.

I put it up for sale and it was sold in four days. I went to look at the penthouse I am in now, burst into tears and told myself that it was ridiculous that I was now about to live in an apartment.

I mean how would they all carry the coffin in the lift?

For some reason, I went back the next day and saw it for what it was. I don't know what changed especially as I had always been able to see the potential in an area. It is what I did. Maybe, because it was about to be *my* area that my mood was clouded on the first visit. The property I had purchased previously was business. This was the business of life.

I am a gut instinct person – which makes it odd I didn't fancy it at first. But when I went back, I knew it was the right thing to do. This was the only way to make a new start.

So, I moved in with a girlfriend for a few days, sent the removal company to the old house to pack up and left them to it, moving in in July 2017. I got rid of everything. I new I had to start afresh.

Around me today – these four walls.

Many people with depression or anxiety or loneliness use that phrase to reflect their misery. I do so to mark my joy. They are my four walls. They reflect me and support me. I don't look at them and see deceit back. Deliberately and everywhere I turn, there is a sign of the good elements in my life. I don't want to say that there is a symbol of everything that I have achieved because it is vulgar to brag but what I do see in every corner and on every surface is something that is hard-earned and represents me. Even the bowls in the cupboard have their unique stamp of myself on them and that makes me proud.

It has been *the* best thing I ever did – bar having my children. It is a good investment but I don't see it as financial for once. I rate it as the value I have finally learned to place in me.

The torment has been huge. It broke me.

My safety net was cut. That rope that I saw as security had in fact strangled me. Wriggling free is the only point you understand that. In that process of escaping – without knowing that flight was the only way because you perceived that the marriage was your stability – you get so far before your feet get caught in that very netting and the rope begins to strangle you a little before you climb free once more.

One step forward, two steps back.

Mostly, I see in my new property, a home.

Filled with me.

I am starting to understand through the décor that I create that in fact I can worry a little less. I am self-sufficient and I am will get through today and rise again tomorrow, and no the business will not disappear at the speed my angst deluded me it could.

Far from it.

I am in the best place I have ever been.

30 years – 23 with Roger. Gone. Time to build a new future that reflected me, who I was and who I am and my success, making every statement around me to remind myself of what made me tick when in effect the clock was standing still. I wouldn't of course get there overnight.

I never went back. However Roger parked himself about 100 metres away in a rented flat with an internet replacement. That helped. Who in their right mind would break free and pitch themselves on their ex-wife's doorstep? This was an episode of *Cold Feet*!

Leaving *was* a massive wrench as ruthlessly as I exited – the kids had grown up there in what I believed to be the happiest of times yet it had to be done. It felt strange but liberating. *Now*, despite that being my perception that they were 'the happiest of times', the girls tell me that this feels more of a home.

Whilst this was a major step to finding me again, I was still struggling.

When your kids are telling you get some help then you know it is time to listen. Despite the counselling and therapy over the years, this was new territory.

I could go back to those people and places but it didn't feel right. There was too much of the past in those conversations and I really wanted somebody to get me out of this and take me forward.

I was desperate for someone to wave a magic wand. I needed a fairy godmother. Where was my genie in a bottle?

In fact her name was Jenny.

In October 2015, I was organising a Bar Mitzvah. It was a bittersweet day for a hostess who had sadly lost her daughter and was celebrating her son becoming a man.

On such cruel moments someone else's life can also turn. Some stuff does happen for a reason and I know better than anyone how a seating plan or a random encounter at an event can change the course of people's lives.

And there she was. A lady, whom I had not seen for many years, comes to greet me.

'You need to come and see me, ' she said as though she had been watching over me.

I had indeed tried the odd medium in the past. Odd, as in more than one, rather than strange.

She seemed to know everything. That does not mean the infidelity, the websites, the texts…they were just props in the game. She had an intuition that was able to connect within my heart in a way that nobody else would come close to. Her instinct that day was that I was in trouble. She might have heard the odd thing around town about my marriage – that didn't matter. She was drawn to me without me seeking her out. I don't think this meeting was chance. Probably, I had given up looking.

So, I did what you would expect.

I ignored her for six months!

In the end, I couldn't any more. Part of the problem was that it just wasn't going away. More and more people were coming out of the woodwork. That Christmas, just before I was to leave on holiday, I opened the post one morning.

I get so much mail – most of it nonsense – that I normally bulldoze my way through it. However something stopped me dead in my tracks.

A picture of Roger was staring back at me.

From his match.com profile. His pseudonym was Jay 64 – his son's name and year of birth.

Attached was a note.

'If your husband is looking for a match, perhaps remove his picture to avoid the embarrassment.'

Total and utter humiliation.

Imagine starting your day with that.

Somebody was either scorned by him or was doing me a favour. Either they were part of his world or were seriously looking out for mine and had decided enough was enough. I was still in denial. Everything comes out in the end.

So then, perhaps thinking I could do this on my own and realising otherwise, I called her.

Out of desperation.

It is easy to say that I would not be here now if it weren't for Jenny. Unless you are truly determined to take your own life and my God I nearly gave it a go one night, then there is often a way out of these situations. For me, Jenny was the escape route and the empowerment to move on without damage – and that is the key.

You can get better in stages and wake up years later and realise you are there, that you have made it out of the woods. But can you ever be the same again or indeed *better,* without constantly looking back and feeling damaged and worthless?

The answer is yes with the right help.

I am here to tell the tale.

Of course, I had to go to hell and back first.

There were two key elements to my therapy.

Jenny allowed me to think my crazy thoughts. She created an atmosphere of calm in my mad world so I could be unhappy, suicidal, angry – any negative emotion and that level-headed tranquillity never wavered. She was my punch bag while I was not boxing clever.

But she also took me right back to basics. It was her who made me understand that my relationship with the girls was suffering. She helped me become a parent again when I didn't even realise that I had regressed into being their child.

Part of that process was that she tapped into Dad.

Whilst we had more than reconciled towards the end of his life, it left so many regrets and lessons which I had made little attempt to understand and foolishly could very well end up making the same mistakes if I still chose to do so.

'Your father is guiding me,' she told me caringly on our second session one dark autumnal Friday night.

The setting could not have been more grim.

I had given her very little to go on.

She kept banging on about Dad, as though she was getting a message.

What on earth did she mean?

'Your father was with us,' she told me.

And I had total trust in her. I had no reason not to but as part of the repair mechanism within you, you either become suspicious of everything or you place it all in their hands. I was that low *plus* I did trust her.

'He is mentioning a photo,' she pressed me gently.

This was quite an extraordinary development and whilst I shrugged it off at the time, it sat with me and took me a week to think about.

I had never had a photo of Dad in the old house and it drove him mad. At least, if I didn't want him up staring back at me, the girls had a right to see their grandfather. The more he would mention it when alive, the more determined I was not to put one up.

So that bit of it made sense.

Yet, it is when I moved that this is key. When the removal guys had delivered everything to my new pad and I finally had the strength and energy to unpack and begin the process of cleansing my soul and finding the new me, laying on the top inside the first box was a picture of Mum and Dad on their wedding day.

I smiled at the time and did make it the first photo in my new home. I had to get through so much stuff unpacking that I didn't think much more of it until Jenny told me that she was picking it up.

Divorce literally had opened a lot of boxes.

I would never have put it on my piano. That was my first strike of rebellion at four years old. That is where I placed it and it still stands. Slowly but surely, I began to realise that actually what I now had was more than I did previously.

In Dad's death but principally through Jenny, I understood more and with clarity and it now gives me comfort and security. It re-established my own relationship with my kids where I had often felt that I was *both* parents to them but now they had taken on that role. I look at nonsense and know that I lost it when my daughter went away for a month to France and got her tongue pierced then could barely speak when I called her so I reacted by grounding her.

Yet it was her that told me that Roger was a sociopath and it was not actually me that broke the relationship. It just took five years to realise it whilst I was still in it.

My emotions remained numb. I would see Jenny every week and sometimes we would go backwards before we would go forward. And we hadn't really even begun to talk about my marriage.

37 Cushion The Blame

'I thought he held me on a pedestal,' I confessed to Jenny.

That was not the arrogant me thinking that I was something or someone. It was just the craving, I suppose, even to be idolised…perhaps seeking that paternal love but mistakenly thinking it was coming in the shape of a husband.

'He may have done but when on a pedestal you can only go one way,' she replied.

This was the beginning of a long and painful process, in which I had to go right back to even go forward a little.

It is ironic really that Roger and I began counselling *together* in 2009 because we couldn't find peace with his own fifteen year-old daughter. Christmas holidays – that one time of year when families were meant to cut off and be together – were just awful. She wouldn't engage at all. So, we sought guidance to manage that relationship and help him but he wasn't engaged as a father at all. Things were so bad that she wouldn't even come to my daughter's wedding.

The process that began so we could be one as a 'modern' family of many parts ends up with me alone in tears in the chair piecing it all together and working out where the lies begun and ended – if indeed they ever stopped at all. I am tempted to conclude that, in attempting to talk through situations and emotions about his own child, I gave him a sense of how it all worked so by the time that it came to us, he was well prepared in the process and could churn out any old bullshit.

So, by 2010, when I asked him in front of the counsellor if he had ever been unfaithful to me and to swear on his daughter's life, he looked me in the eye and said he hadn't.

When I went for dinner with a friend of mine who owned a furniture chain I found out at that he had bought two silk cushions for a woman 'and not to tell Liz'…it was a thunderbolt but one which I still allowed him to recover from. All the time he was contributing a paltry amount to the housekeeping, I just assumed that he was putting money away whilst I was investing in property. He wasn't of course. Soon, the small details outweighed the big ones. After all, the infidelity was just big one whopper on its own, but the cushions, and the golf and the text messages – they were just multiple offences belonging to somebody who could not tell the truth.

Jenny was the only person who struck the true connection with me. Clearly the timing was right too when I bumped into her but at one point I had been seeing both Relate and a specialist in London. I was desperate for answers.

It really is what you put into these sessions that determines what you get out – once you are emotionally receptive enough to process it all, and that does take time. Emotionally receptive can also equal emotionally desperate. I was rock bottom and therefore ready when I met Jenny.

If you are not willing to recognise sincerely that this is the last chance saloon and your stance is just to go through the motions with counselling, rather pacifying before you are out of the woods so you can start your little seedy world again in a few months time, then you are never going to get anywhere in life.

On one occasion I had walked in on Roger having a Facetime counselling session with his specialist and I realised that in fact, he was not repairing or willing to learn but instead using the counsellor as a confidante to his next plot:

'Let her go to Dubai and think about it while she is away,' I overheard. 'See if you want to move out while she is away.'

Wait a minute. I am due to be speaking in the U.A.E. He is supposed to be reconciling. But all is he doing is buying himself time on his exit strategy. Our Altrincham flat, which was supposed to be being renovated was being readied once more to be the bachelor flat.

I cancelled the conference in Dubai. I rarely did that – nor could I allow work to be getting distracted or derailed by the what was going on. On this occasion, I succumbed.

When you look back, you see clearly that these were moments when it was way past all over but you carry on, continuing to put plasters on a wound where stitches and surgery were required.

I had always said too that 'if he ever fucks around, he's out of here' and my track record would back up that mentality except for the first time in my life my actions did not.

I was no longer that person and I must have said to so many friends who also knew that at that point I was also lying. I just didn't know it. Many of the people in my world of course only really knew the persona and not the person.

Too busy in the hamster wheel of life going round and round, I saw nothing and then when it was too late wondered why I hadn't seen it fifteen years previously. I needed to grow up.

Anger soon subsides; sadness prevails. In truth, I was devastated that I hadn't made it to a silver wedding anniversary. I probably could have done but it would have just perpetuated the lie. I had huge regrets that despite the kids, despite the success of the business, despite the financial rewards, I still had not had a lengthy stable relationship that lasted. It was the only aspect of my life that I failed to control.

As you look outward on to this mess, you look back inward and really despite that control and confidence, I was needy and very insecure – undoubtedly a product of my upbringing, a double-edged sword that made me who I was professionally but left me all at sea personally.

If I had half the common sense I had in business in my personal life, I would be almost there. I accept that many of my character flaws have caused me unhappiness in my personal life. Yet, I have learned that you are not actually weak if you are vulnerable and yet I worried about this most days after I left as I picked up the pieces.

I knew the worth of my personal brand but did stress over my public face being tarnished and people would think that the mask had come off. The reality was the opposite. I am sure Roger has his circle who will say the kind of stuff that people do come out with like 'the bitch got what she deserved' but amongst my own, people came forward and nobody was surprised from his clients to his 'close' friends. That technique of attracting victim status to masquerade your own tracks was right at the core of his armoury. Then I learned about the inappropriate emails to the woman at Bury Football Club.

187

He couldn't help himself.

It has taken me time to understand but I realise now that he simply wanted somebody to end the marriage. This in itself is extraordinary. Every instinct that he pursued was of a man who was constantly setting himself free. He behaved with so much freedom and yet he couldn't be the one to seize it.

Words constantly rung in my ears and only after the end did I understand the double bluffs that I had taken as truth:

None more so than this:

'Why on earth did you marry me?' I once asked him.

'I wanted a woman with a house,' he answered.

I thought he had been joking.

Welcome to my new reality. All the things you took for granted were now halved. Simple every day tasks had to factor in just the one person not two – from basic stuff like food and diaries to more emotionally testing criteria such as attending functions or going on holiday. Who would have thought going abroad to chill alone could be so troubling?

I, of course, had attended many events over the years on my own and in a work capacity. Two key points – being alone and knowing that you have something to go back to puts an entirely different perspective on that moment when it might just be you there. An event in London and an early train back to the family home has purpose and you have the security to know it is there. Take all that away and you can really ask yourself what the point is.

Equally, you can be out and about a work do and lose yourself in it at the expense of facing the reality of the mess you were in. I don't think I necessarily feared the solitude and isolation but that solitude and isolation only magnified the point that I was in a big mess, and despite my full-on work face and attitude, one that I really did not think I deserved to be in.

So, there is a difference between being alone and loneliness – but the former accentuated the latter because of the time and space it gave you to process and second-guess the gaps in your knowledge in the ever-unfolding mis-adventures of a partner.

That meant also that one date loomed large on the horizon. What was I going to do at Christmas?

Why did I even worry? I mean – it had been miserable the previous year. It was essentially just another day or week on the calendar. Of course, it said family and yes, if you weren't happy there should be a sense of peace and calmness in the air at that time of year. It was not the time of year to be miserable or at each other's throats.

I knew I had to get away.

189

So when I was invited by a long-standing client and friend to Barbados, I nervously accepted. I did dither for a moment then graciously agreed.

I knew, that I would be well looked-after and in good company. I would have time to myself and get some sun on my back and there would be a structure which meant that I wouldn't go rudderless – abroad and alone.

My friend spent December in Oliver Messel's house – the English artist and one of the foremost stage designers of the 20th century. It was steeped in history – Princess Margaret had stayed there. He also owned the hottest restaurant on the island. Can you think of a better place to hang out over Christmas?

I needed that routine too – up for breakfast almost by order at eight, lunch at one, afternoon tea at four, drinks at seven and dinner at eight. There was no time to linger and ponder. Life was rich and full.

My standards and time-keeping slipped a little as the holiday went on. Maybe I was drifting with my thoughts or perhaps just starting to relax. One day, I was late for the afternoon tea after a 4.15 massage. I showed up in a t-shirt with all my greasy hair. Not the best!

Detox also meant clearing out my system of the emotional demons too of course.

And that was the day Simon Cowell happened to be there with his wife Lauren! Of all the times to never get that opportunity to make a first impression again, this was one of them as he shook my hand with me looking akin to Miss Haversham. He must have wondered who I was even though we had of course mutual friends such as Gary Barlow and the showbiz agent Jonathan Shalit.

But hey, I have seen some of those high waistbands that Simon has made his name over the years so I don't think he was about to judge. The problem for me is that I am an opportunist and everything *is* an opportunity, despite the fact that I was actually supposed to be switching off and relaxing for the first time in years. Yes, sometimes I have to be reined in but these moments come and go instantly. Simon was always in Barbados after a long season of the British *X Factor* and whatever else he was working on at the time. Everybody's guard was down. There was probably never an easier time to make a contact.

I loved him. I thought he was charming and I could see a driving force in Lauren Silverman behind him and an admiration for my host. He was – dare I say it – normal and of course, the 'club' was in full force here. Nobody was looking over their shoulder. Success and mutual respect brought them together.

Whilst I am in Barbados, Gary Barlow calls. He does not know that I am there – nor does he need his PA to ring me anymore.

He and Dawn cannot get a table at the Lone Star Hotel and Restaurant. It was built in the 1940s as a garage. Originally, it was the only place on the island licensed to sell petrol. The new owner has put money in and turned it into a six bedroomed coral stone property with its own access to the beach.

Gary and Dawn needed feeding!

I tell him that I will sort it. I always back myself to get a table and I know that full never means full.

I am with the owner and get them in.

It is nice to be able to help out and be the person at the end of the line trusted to help facilitate something for people who have enriched your life over the years.

Equally, I begin to understand that there is a great feeling in helping people without any deal needing to be part of it.

This is called friendship.

I am no longer angry. I will not waste one more day of my life to that spent emotion. These, though, are not just my words.

I met up with an old friend whom I hadn't seen in an eternity and these are the kind of people who serve you well because they bookend who you were and who you are. They measure the distance of the journey.

'You're not angry any more,' she told me without prompting.

But I know that she meant all over and not just specifically about Roger.

It hadn't dawned on me that my work image might seem thus. Angry – I hadn't really considered. Tough and as hard as nails, independent and successful yes and ruthless in delivering but only now can I see that I left some people reeling and asking 'what's up with her?'

It had taken me four years to get to these conclusions. That is how long I spent clearing up the mess within me in the aftermath. That I am even able to write this at all tells me that I have said goodbye to the worst of it.

Of course, some will draw the usual conclusions that it is therapeutic to put it all down but I have to rule that out. The therapy was *therapeutic* – believe it or not – and it was that which cleared the way for the here and now. I have already long since arrived here before I even wrote the words 'Chapter 1'.

Where do I stand now?

Grateful.

He did me the most massive of favours – to remind me of what I have got and to understand what I lost. By the latter, I mean that in the same way that taking to counselling led us into Roger's infidelities, his deceit led me to explore Dad and therefore me. Through the back door, I heal.

I am at peace with myself. I understand my father now and whilst I cannot change the past, I realise the mistakes, borne out of the characters we were.

'Your father knew everything…and a lot more,' Jenny would say.

I accept that.

So, when he warned me about the men I was marrying, he was aware that Michael, for example, was in the trouble, and gave me a gentle nudge, but was smart enough too that I had to find out for myself and make my own mistakes. That is part of being a parent, isn't it?

Looking back, I understand that he knew *everything* even when I thought he didn't as a fourteen year old on a Saturday night. Where do you draw the line between over-parenting and therefore the risk of alienation, and protective parenting because you know your child is about to mess up?

He allowed me to fall which I think was both his natural style and a sad admission that he had also messed up…that he parented in such a way that meant we weren't close and he knew because of that, he only had the right to go so far.

This young adult making mistakes wouldn't have listened when marrying the wrong man. The adult today would take an extra moment and hear Dad's warnings…then probably proceed anyway!

That is what the therapy brought — clarity of thought to that relationship, which dare I say it, began to flourish after his death and only through the work with Jenny.

I have dated a little since. But guess what? I am happy in my own skin.

That skin needs a beach tan and quite a bit of plastic around it but learning to live with yourself is not necessarily the hardest thing to achieve but I do think it is one of the greatest symbols of recovery and self-awareness.

The person who was gutted that they didn't fulfil society's expectations of making it to a silver wedding anniversary was also bloody relieved they could come home to their own space and pour themselves a large vodka and know that their diary was full and their life was rich and there was still plenty of time and life ahead.

I am in that place.

There is a fine line between going back to an empty place at night and it swallowing you up, staring at the phone and wondering 'why me?' to thriving and building a new you from that very tranquillity.

I was never in that situation and way past it because the business and the girls were so much of my life. Now, coming out of the other side of the therapy, I realise I had a scare which is no bad thing because there is no way in the world I will ever go back there.

The fall out from my turmoil is not romance or finance. It is nothing to do with him. It was my wake up call.

My relationships are better than ever. With everybody.

I don't really date any more though one flirtation did say 'You come with a government health warning'! Even that though – I am well aware is based on professional reputation, and that is the key to much of this story.

None of my clients would know that I was going through mental torture for about four years. I was perfectly able to turn up, wear a smile and deliver for them. In fact, if you look at some of the work and much of the media that I have done it is during this period. So you can say, if you like, here is a person who can turn it on autopilot or you can be me, and real and look in that mirror. What do I see?

The reflection shows that my team carried me and that business is better than ever. Years of being tough had set the blueprint for the company and yet, when I was not quite there but still just about, my staff stepped up and over-delivered.

I am grateful.

That appreciation is both for the moment and for the future because through their work ethic and integrity, I raised mine and without ever getting close to taking a back seat, I was finally able to let go and delegate.

It *had* been my way or the highway. Eamonn, in his kind foreword to this book has that wrong! But, if my dear friend perceives that it wasn't then I have done well to hide behind that mask. Now the path was clear for their ideas and a carte blanche trust that meant that my 8 am strops were gone if something didn't happen.

I must have been firing on all professional cylinders despite the emotional tank being empty. In 2016, somehow I managed to book Ed Sheeran for what I believe to be his only gig that year. As I said, some of my best work was done during this time. A charity event for the East Anglia Children's Hospice, Ed stormed the Natural History Museum. I joined the other dinosaurs in the room.

There were days when I couldn't function, might have brought the business down if I were alone and persuaded myself that nothing else mattered and had continued down that road towards a very lame attempt at suicide but the truth is I got through and I come out the other side so relieved, so happy, so enriched, so focussed but so much better a boss and friend.

I could have just gone off round the world at a moment's notice. I did India with my friends – my way! I didn't at this point have the emotional connection with anything and was still numb so what would have been the point in pretending I was 18 and backpacking across Australia, or riding an elephant through Sri Lanka? I could have bought a one way ticket to anywhere and gone for as long as I wanted but in fact in doing that I would only be in the fast lane to hell and back. Escaping only papers over the cracks you leave behind.

I had come full circle but was now in my sixties. To flee would ultimately mean that I would return at some point and the unanswered questions would remain. They would still be there waiting for me, and as it transpired, sticking around meant that faded acquaintances were able to finally come forward and help me piece together the gaps. I wouldn't have learned half of what I know now if I had been waiting for Krakatoa to erupt. It was tough but better to be at home to feel the tremors still registering on the Richter Scale.

The truth sets you free.

Plus, one inner piece of steel served me well. The business saved me and the people in the business did so. I had built this up from nothing at a time when people didn't believe it possible often against the backdrop of playing that role of both parents, and certainly always being the breadwinner – and always working out of my office as a toilet! Never forget where you came from.

One of the darkest of days when the rain fell and deluged you in autumn grim that compounded the tears which had flooded your restless night time slumber of the churning mind, one voice spoke louder and clearer than ever.

You are not going to give this away.

You never expect anything on a plate in life – except piano lessons at the age of four – but the lottery of life meant that as my world self destructed and fell apart, my 'competitors' were getting their act together. And then I lost one of my staff after eleven years, which added to the abandonment and feelings of being let down. I don't know if she could see that maybe I wasn't quite on it at that point or if it was just time for her.

Another departed for Dubai after eight years with me.

I took both personally without any reason to do so. They are entitled to make changes to their lives. They probably helped too. It is one thing knowing you are clinging on but just about getting away with it. If one or two people jump ship then it should be a sign to turn it around – and fast.

Look at my language there – 'jump ship' as though all around me were reaching for the lifeboats. This is not how I really think at all but would have been in that moment when everything was bringing me down. They were more than free to try pastures new. They were in charge of their lives.

But the me, me, me at the time can only see that as rejection and another sign that the wheels were coming off. They weren't. The mind plays tricks.

But it is true that around me, everybody suddenly wanted to be a wedding planner now. I had a great reputation for delivering (and as 'angry' to others!) but to some I was older, expensive and intimidating. I could see that people might prefer a younger operative with their million followers on YouTube and find them easier to negotiate with.

It took four years to move from constantly having this gremlin on my back dumping shit at my door every week to gradually looking back over my shoulder and seeing it wasn't there any more.

196

I could go to work and wander if into some Narnia type illusion of a fantasyland and then come home to the four walls and the little monkey would return, like a huge back pack weighing my shoulders down. I would often wake in tears and that meant the gremlin was still with me. Bit by bit, my existence went from hanging by a thread to being there less and less but it probably took until the summer of 2018 before I really set *it* and myself free again.

I felt a failure but I knew I had obligations to my kids, my staff and my clients that – daytime, at least – I couldn't wallow in it.

As the gremlin haunted me less and less, I began to restructure, handing over more and more responsibility but importantly for the girls in the office, acknowledging that they were more than capable without me, even though there would never be the *without me* scenario.

I gave the credit they deserved for the first time.

If it had not been for this volcano in my life randomly spewing its venomous lava everywhere, I would have still been in an office where four lines would ring at once and I would be controlling all the calls. I also knew that the best blueprint for progression was to learn from the younger person's world with the changing market and the power of social media and to combine that with the experience and creativity that had been at our heart since day one. My understanding of team was paramount.

My vision, therefore, was to strike the balance between allowing TLC to support me without losing or relinquishing control. Half eight to half five was out – delivering with the same sense of responsibility remained.

But, I know that my marriage fiasco opened up that Pandora's Box. I could have found out much later in life with less life ahead to live. Billy big shot had the wool pulled right over her eyes. That's the struggle – seeing in terms of business whilst being blind to it in your personal life.

I never saw any of it coming. And yet, still I continued to piece the jigsaw together. I found it he was still benefitting from my perks without my permission – heavenly knows for whom – and worse, the biggest own-goal on the planet for which he should know better was still to come.

He had acquired Eamonn's number without my knowledge and had been texting to see if Ruth could get him backstage at *Strictly Come Dancing* on BBC1 where she was now competing.

Clearly, the answer would be no. I don't know what possessed him to fire off that text but even I have never had such high levels of self-belief to think the answer might actually be yes.

Eamonn has very high morals and told me straightaway.

Lawyers successfully stepped in.

In short, it became the only thing in 60 years that I could not control.

On the other side, I am now more in control than ever.

It is true.

What doesn't kill you makes you stronger.

There are three weeks to go before the opening.

It is now 2018.

One of London's most iconic brands is coming to the ever-evolving Spinningfields in Manchester.

Can I come for a meeting?

Few people intimidate me. Richard Caring, a very feared social entrepreneur, wants to see me. Caring by name, less so by nature?!

I stand next to this formidable man. I am but four feet away.

'What do you mean you do events?' he begins.

He has obviously been placed in this conversation with a PA. This is not his detail. He just wants it perfect and wants it done.

The clock is ticking and they are not happy in the slightest with what they already have in place. This is simply not good enough for this legendary brand.

He walks towards me, shakes my hand and doesn't look at me.

I have seen this type before. I flash back to the Isle of Man and know I have to find a different way.

There is a lot at stake.

Can I rescue the opening of The Ivy?

The lead in time is so short I tell them that they have to change the days. I can't do the Wednesday or Thursday that they have earmarked for that week. If they want me it will have to move. And so it does!

But I still can't crack this man.

Then it happens. I find the Achilles Heel.

'Nothing lasts forever,' he tells me when I confirm I am a party planner as though disbelieving that this is actually my job!

'Herpes does,' I reply.

He laughs and then laughs some more.

I don't think I touched a nerve and he had inside knowledge of that virus! As always I used an intimidating situation to my advantage by fighting my way out of the box. The game changed in an instant. I suspect he wasn't used to anyone taking him on, probably rarely used to be challenged and quite likely to getting his own way.

My black humour often cut the ice.

It made people sit up and listen. I never saw any point in being a wallflower. That first meeting is always the benchmark to how fruitful the relationship will be. In short, you have to be prepared to lose to win. You go in big with balls and if you lose you must conclude that it wasn't right for you because you are going to get the blame if the night is a disaster. You can measure that from the off. So if you are not working with somebody who, by and large, isn't prepared to do things the way you 'suggest' then it probably is not worth doing at all.

It *is* my way or the highway. Even if you are Richard Caring.

I suspect too that, whilst people around sometimes feel they should be, that in a situation like this he doesn't want a yes man. Yes men teach you nothing when you go to somebody specific like me for advice. You have to lead and from that they take confidence and respect.

And in terms of my character this is where I am most misinterpreted.

I know people say I am difficult. It generally means that I do different and that I have nailed it.

Now, for the Ivy, there are Ivy standards and I would allow myself a little leeway in being led by them but with the launch just three weeks away. I had to take on the role nobody else could so I wasn't building two tier stages, enchanted castles, yellow brick roads, and sweeping staircases – their need for creativity was less.

That is the side of my work that people quote and remember but they forget that every party comes with a huge set of logistics – not least the time frame involved here. So, they laid down the blueprint which had to be in keeping with The Ivy brand and therefore required less influence from me but they

200

needed someone to pull it all together. It had to look like The Ivy and not a nightclub. I didn't want to be creating a grotto on the third floor. I needed to deliver their brand bang on – a subtle difference from many corporate bashes where the client wanted to show off to staff and their own customers something that was beyond their brand and into the make believe but at the centre of which I always left clever reminders as to whose party it was. This was different. I had to deliver their brand.

'Will it be any good?' Richard asked.

'It will be mega,' I bluffed, backing myself as always without knowing how.

Again – radiate confidence, mistake it for arrogance if you like. But most of all, and every single time, make the client realise you get it and you get them.

I delivered a few me touches – obviously. The odd flame and snake charmer, a few Elvisses, a *green* red carpet in keeping with their brand but also to be different and podium dancers masquerading as trees which came to life as the stars arrived to a rousing bongo drum set outside on the street which meant that, if you weren't part of it, you soon knew about it. Take the party to the streets – a fantastic way of creating curiosity, word of mouth and a little envy.

Your entry made a statement.

Inside, the décor said The Ivy. The right thing was to leave this alone and add special touches. Stay on brand.

A gleaming golden hallway with a marble effect floor magnified by a gilded ceiling and mirrored walls. It looked high class.

But I really had to think on my feet. It was unusual at home that I had to cut through so much red tape. Expect that in Moscow or Marrakesh yes, but think about the centre of Manchester whether you know the place well or not.

It is a standard city centre skyline. Every day a new building is going up. The main drag, Deansgate, which runs across Spinningfields takes about fifteen minute to drive along when it only runs for a mile or so.

It is the best place ever for a party to take centre stage and just about the worst to unload and set up.

And that was part of their problem

We have got double yellow lines outside. I bulldozed my way through. The council, for some awkward reason won't let you put a generator there.

I put a generator there.

I needed about 10,000 square feet back of house to prepare. There was nowhere to go. I knocked on an office block adjacent and simply asked. They duly obliged. I was just thinking on my feet and being practical. I was out of options and out of time.

Most importantly, could I deliver an A list guest list so that the brand had that elite Ivy appeal about it. You know the reputation – 'the stars go there' and even they struggle to get a table. That had to be the message.

In essence, they were buying my brain and my little black book.

Years of contacts and producing events like this meant that one phone call would be all it took. The *Manchester Evening News* would definitely stick this somewhere near their front cover and others would follow. That is job done. That is public relations. To know with concrete certainty that you can pull off the event inside the venue but then have the client waking up to front page coverage the next day is the complete package. They knew I could deliver and so did I.

So, as you might expect the usual suspects came out to play – all the young ones from Corrie and Emmerdale took to the red carpet as did the chef and *Strictly* star Simon Rimmer and your obvious Manchester United boys – Ryan Giggs and Phil Neville in amongst the good and the great.

For them, an exclusive night, and of course, a chance to keep profiles high should they wish. There are so many opportunities these days to show other sides of your character through social media, reality TV and dare I say it – the opening of an envelope – that, as much as people in this field craved their privacy, they also valued their own brand and whilst you could play the same character in Corrie for 40 years, it was nice to get asked to do other things and to not be seen as a one trick pony. Attending an event like this put you out there.

Worse though – to not be invited to the opening of the brand that in London would regularly host David Beckham and Tom Cruise was essentially a faux-pas. The stars knew it and the brand knew it.

And they wanted tables there in the future too.

Most importantly, when you have checked with the venue after the event and your read the press and you know it has gone down a storm, you are only looking to hear one phrase.

'Everybody who is anybody was there'.

And they were.

I learnt from it too. The new me was evolving. That awful passage of time had obviously let to a journey of self-discovery within the real me, but like many people who recover from – let's call it a trauma – it spills over into everything you do and everything you are.

You find a little more time to thank people when you realise how thankful *you* are for what you have got. You delegate because you trust and you see how your staff have carried you and that is different from barking orders because you need a dogsbody. You attach value to the tasks you are assigning because you are seeing people as that rather than as part of your machine gun scatterbrain lifestyle. You actually listen a little rather than selectively tuning into the bits you need to hear. There is a major difference. Significantly too, your overview of the business changes.

Is this really what I want for the rest of my life?

Yes – it is but I want a little bit more. I want to do more TV, more lecturing, more consultancy. I want to be less hands-on without resisting lending more than a hand.

Yet, it is in your nature to *never* take both hands of the wheel. Recently, I told my staff that I would now be having every Friday off unless there was an event. It was time for me.

That lasted a week.

Business is booming. That is why. And I am back.

At what point then do you say, 'do you know what, I am going to do those bucket list trips??' My brain remains young, many of my body parts are younger than my grandchildren, but let's face facts, we are all on borrowed time!

And the business is changing and one thing I definitely learnt from The Ivy is that businesses were starting to call me as much for the party as for whom I could bring to it.

I had added value – no need to question my worth. Though, of course, it hasn't been easy getting there. It is a lifetime of work. That first number I ever wrote down and kept in my little black book somewhere back in the 1980s now sits alongside thousands of others. You don't get here overnight and you are still getting here every single day.

So, from The Ivy came *that* understanding and it takes me straight to Cos. Collection of Style – literally. Cos is a young, unique, stylish, Swedish brand, owned by H and M. My daughter loves it. They were about to move into St Ann's Square in Manchester where the former Gap shop had stood before it moved on to the Arndale Centre.

This was seen as massive news for Manchester – Debenhams was on its knees and the iconic Kendals store which had stood in the city centre since 1832 was no more. Their arrival was a huge message to retail.

Now here is the interesting thing. I tendered for the contract to run the opening. I don't like that process and I rarely submit to it but business is business and it was a decent contract.

I did not get the deal.

Then they called me.

I guess that is an implication that they weren't quite getting the full package. A pattern was starting to form here – could I provide fifteen or so high net worth business people and around ten celebs for the opening?

They didn't want me anymore. They needed my contacts.

I gave them half of Corrie as usual. Front page guaranteed.

Of course, there is a risk if you are new to this that you can promise a person will attend and they themselves will say 'yeah yeah yeah, I will be there definitely' and then on the day, the texts start in the morning saying they are not feeling so well or they have childcare issues, or they have been called in late but of course, I have heard this all before.

'Don't tell me you are not coming because you are,' I would kill their disinclination in one swift phone call!

And if they protest further then I would invariably follow up with 'I will send a car, get there for the photo shoot and then go home' but by that point it would rarely come to that and if it did, guess what? Once they were there, they would end up staying anyway.

It works both ways and it evens itself out over the years. You have to have the relationship and network to be able to promise a star-studded turn-out without fear of compromise of a no-show. At some point, one of these guys will ring me for a table here or a favour there and they know they are calling because I can pull it off so nobody is storing up favours but there is a silent trust that if I ask you to show, it is good news for everyone and will be repaid.

When I look back at the Cos opening and look forward to the future of my consultancy, I realise that this is the pay off for years of hard work and networking and that perhaps one future for the party planner lies in providing the clientele rather than for the client per se.

You see – I got paid more for arranging the people than I would have done if I had arranged the party.

41 The Party Is Over…

Well not quite. I am not sure it will ever be.

In my kind of world, you are never quite done. I thought I could see a time when I might retreat, but one is never going to stop taking a phone call from Gary Barlow or Eamonn Holmes or chipping in with more than an idea when the time finally comes to take a backseat. My life has been my work and my work has been my life.

As you have read.

So, for all the blurred lines between personal disasters and getting paid to make fun for people, the other side of that is, that when it comes time to stop, those lines remain grey areas and you just never switch off. Plus, you have been committed for several years to certain charities with clients like Marina Dalglish, and whilst individuals and organisations know that it is a massive team effort to pull off their night, I know that they buy into me and that I will always be the face of the business to them.

Repeat customers like Marina will only stop when age defeats them! By nature then, I am always involved even if I decide to call it a day!

Ironically, I write this in the autumn of 2019 when business has never been better and more to the point, nor have I. I note that more and more events are coming in last minute or relatively so. A sign of the times and the economy. People's expectations are greater and the uncertainty of the era means often that they are rushed, mulling over whether they can afford the budget, not knowing where a Brexit UK sits economically but then just deciding to go for it. It is disconcerting but I rise to every challenge. I have the security of my little black book, which I know can make most things happen once people sign on the dotted line. But, I still need time to plan.

Today, for example, four leads from a key corporate client, two Indian weddings and a high profile 50th birthday party together with a leading international hotel for Christmas décor!

Valuable relationships that have lasted years and lasted well. I am grateful and always energised by it all.

They have a giant Ferris wheel going in the car park at the Trafford Centre. Can I dress it for Halloween?

Why not?

Potentially, this is the ultimate Health and Safety nightmare. Get this right and everybody who shops at one of Europe's busiest shopping centres will tell somebody. Get it wrong and you will be hanging like the skeleton, swinging from the rafters!

There are 36 pods to decorate. I start with a speaking skeleton in each of them. They are expecting something different. Then I add cobwebs and spiders. You have to take care over the effects of lighting. You need to spell out the risks to pregnant women and those with epilepsy etc. People often ignore them but you have to be watertight. I can't put fabric in the pod because of the fire risk. The paperwork is taking days. And so it goes on with health and safety tightly on their broomsticks!

I also have a Question and Answer session at Manchester University. I would not have the confidence to mentor students if I had not survived the previous few years. Most importantly, happy in my skin over the last two, not quite post therapy, learning to delegate and trust my team implicitly means I am ready to parent the next generation. It has taken me a long time to realise to myself that if I brought my staff in to do a job then I have to let them do it.

Of course, one of the perks and consequences of having made more than a success of this is that you do then get invited to do more media, TV shows, try out being a columnist, get invited onto boards, meet incredible people and become a keynote speaker.

This autumn I am also invited to become a Non-Executive Director a of a major international fashion brand where I will also offer consultancy. If you like, I have come full circle. Starting out with a Saturday job and working my way through leisure and hospitality, I find myself happily back here. It is all connected. You are never a niche business.

Two key elements keep me here – brand is at the heart of everything I do so even if I am laying on a relatively straightforward staff recognition event, it won't go ahead without plenty of nod and winks to the success of that business such as embroidering their logo onto a coffee cup.

And the vehicle that drives all of this and keeps getting me hired for our business and others is that one piece of magic I wisely started in the year I was married in Liverpool. The little black book.

You never know in life whom you will meet, and perhaps more importantly, when you will meet them again. It is often that second encounter where they want something from you. I have never thrown away a number and one point of access always leads to another – just look at how I wangled that Harry Styles appearance.

So, when people hire me but they can't put down on paper what they are getting for their money, they are often buying the secrets of the little black book. That intangible ingredient that has been the very foundation of my success. Most people have heard of the theory of Six Degrees of Separation (or maybe it is seven, I am never quite sure). I find I rarely need all six.

When people ask me how did I build up all those contacts, the very simple answer is in the question. I valued the necessity of 'it is who you know'.

When you start off in this business you know nobody apart from the young friends you have made in life. You could look around you and think 'well I am never going to get that level…Buckingham Palace, Take That, Pavarotti, Diana Ross, Jon Bon Jovi…' but you get to a point where you are no longer *in* the business but at the centre of it and over time you edge yourself closer to its heart and that means people start to revolve around you rather than the other way round. It makes perfect sense that after over three decades doing this in a place like Manchester and with four major Manchester brands in my DNA in Coronation Street, ITV, Take That and MUFC, the black book is as thriving as ever.

Of course, we live in a world now where we have never had it so easy to connect with people and yet which has also never been so competitive. Somebody reading this today and thinking 'I could do that' probably can make the connections. *But,* can they maintain the connection? Brands and continuing relationships and most importantly referrals via reputation, are built over time even in this most disposable of societies.

I have of course outlived some of my 'customers'. Again, as I write the airline and travel company of over 150 years standing, Thomas Cook is going to the wall. The pioneers of package travel with many customers and staff, in particular, out of Manchester, is no more.

Your next question should be – I guess you have done parties for them too?

And the answer is yes.

They looked after their staff incredibly well but they were beaten in the end as you have seen. I first encountered them through the Crossland family when they ran the old Airtours brand out of a little old industrial town called Helmshore in Lancashire about half an hour out of Manchester. That sold up to the Thomas Cook brand and I had two major tour companies to please.

Thomas Cook, however, through whatever market conditions or management failings does not survive. I say that with no pleasure at all and of course when I reflect on my time working with them, I only associate them with the good times and vice-versa. I went in there to organise motivational and recognition events all over Europe. I knew the brand inside out. I made it my business to be indispensable.

Of course, despite all this experience and the little black book, most people always expect to pay less whilst the multi-millionaires can afford to pay more. But that reflects their own business strategies. It does, however, make you question the value of money. We are dealing all the time in large numbers and what is worth something to one individual has a different association to another.

That applies to me too. Look at my edginess towards my own parties – the ultimate dealmaker has to cut one for herself and finds it too emotionally stressful and justifiable that she hands over the reins!

And when, at the time of writing, I am approached by a leading businessman to become a board member, I am encouraged by words that even I, for all my fronts, need to hear from time to time.

'You have totally underestimated your value and contacts,' he told me.

It sort of blows me away.

Grateful to hear such advice but mindful too that it is one person's insight – albeit a very successful one – I know that I am dealing with somebody who doesn't need written down on paper what I am going to do.

That is a satisfying emotion.

Ultimately, your reputation is all you have. The only thing we all take to the grave is our name. A most valuable inheritance for those we leave behind.

Single, and now a grandmother (Glamama) and comfortable with therapy originally to repair and now to refuel, I can finally look down from the top of the mountain and see how it all happened which is an analysis you are deprived of during the growth of the business as you tread the boards to your destiny!

Throughout all of this, I reflect finally that as hard as I worked, building the business was not *hard* itself. Staying at the top of the game was the difficulty and that essentially reflects the eras and the quality of my suppliers.

For the latter, I have rarely deviated from the brilliant team of people around me who know my standards and have grown themselves creatively by the constant pushing of the bar. For the former, it reflects founding a business in what was not even an industry, branching out in partnership and tackling London, ripping it up and starting again and then fighting the new kid on the block in the social media era which is prepared to undercut you at every corner without having that depth of knowledge or quality that our experience has provided.

I see that today and I am well aware that in the group of students ahead of me, I may well be addressing that person – the new me staring back in my direction.

As I look out this morning on my audience, I see a *few* different versions of me looking back towards the lectern! There is the young M and S girl keen to learn business and a couple of rows in front is the diva who will be first out for a fag to get on her Snapchat.

Generally, I think people come to these events for two reasons. They still can't quite believe to this day that this is a job and that I have made a business out of it. Secondly, everyone loves an entrepreneur story – and that is what essentially I am. Don't be fooled by the ice sculptures and enchanted castles!

Of course, many people are obsessed by fame and want to know all about that and come for gossip but as I was saying to Eamonn and Ruth earlier, I never like to name drop.

I too, very occasionally, get bitten by the bug. I am human. I confess when I found myself in the revolving doors of a hotel in New York and Whitney Houston was coming at me the other way, I continued straight round – and followed the tiny incognito figure into the bar.

On a hen weekend in London, I ran into the actress Helen Mirren – one of my all-time heroes.

'I don't know if I am allowed to speak to you or not,' I mumbled. 'But I think you are great.'

'Of course, you are,' she replied.

No airs and graces. Dead normal.

But there is a marker there. If that had been a business negotiation, I wouldn't have wavered no matter how big the star. I can handle Diana Ross after all. With the mask down and humanity restored, I re-connect with who I am – shy, low on personal confidence and craving a father's approval.

Probably better to keep that mask up.

I am also now media trained and give media training back.

That doesn't mean you will always get it right nor can you always control it. Look at my feelings towards the show *Millionaire Party Planner*.

And PR is as much a part of building this brand as the next party that creates the legend.

Sometimes you can't get it right.

I was asked to help out for the launch of a new charity centre in Widnes. A small do for 80 people became 450 at the Hilton. I managed to pull my old trick of blowing the publicity out of the water by getting *two* names there. Eamonn and Gary Barlow agreed to attend. The next day when I read the article, it didn't look anything like my charity event. In fact, there was no mention of our company – just the charity announcing their new ambassador. Against my better judgement, I had placed my trust in the PR guru for the charity and got bitten as anticipated! That was rare and it goes a little with the territory. You can control, to a degree, but you never know what lies in the head of a sub editor.

But it is very rare that I am going to be on the end of a curveball when it gets to the Q and A. I have heard most of the questions before and back my wit to get me through.

'Have you ever had a disaster?' is an early call from the floor.

'No, plenty of challenges,' is my standard reply.

Moscow, Diana, Remembrance Sunday – challenges, not disasters.

I pay to avert disasters with years of support from quality teams in service industries. I warn them of the dangers of marquees – the effect of water on them or winter...or summer...too hot or too cold or too wet on the approach or above...the need for generators and back-ups and fire exits and how you must never settle for second best just because someone has already busted a gut getting it right in their eyes. I cite the car park at a Budget Insurance do in Peterborough where 1000 people were due and where someone tipped off the fire brigade that I was unintentionally about to breach the regulations of one emergency exit to 120 people.

213

I called the marquee team back and we built new fire exits at the last minute. I sniff out problems before they happen. Experience has taught me what to look for. We have come a long way from no Health and Safety at that first function at The Midland.

Now, it never goes away.

You would be right to ask me if Health and Safety has ever led to an event being called off.

No – but nearly.

You can't postpone the Player of The Year Awards at Liverpool Football Club, can you?

Well, you can if the jobsworth is not happy.

I had erected an elevated seating area. Everybody had known for weeks what was going on. Of course, the H and S police only ever turn up at the last minute, don't they? They even attended the actual evening to check that I was true to my word, forcing me on my hands and knees to tie every chair together to create a flat surface. They made me secure every single cable.

It is difficult to have respect for but there is no point fighting it and I, of course, am responsible for the event, its guests, my team and every supplier. And nobody wants responsibility unless it is a success.

Next question.

'What's the smallest budget you have worked for?' says another.

Interesting how the perception is that I only do big.

'Whatever your budget is, Sir,' is my stock answer.

I enjoy seeing the naivety *and* the spirit of youth. I never went to uni and I tell them this but 'just like you, I swear a lot and like to drink vodka'.

That normally gets a laugh and I suppose is as close as I will get to regrets. It may have all turned out differently. I would have undoubtedly turned out as Dad. Maybe, I did anyway without the gowns and curly wigs. You don't have to have the bit of paper to duplicate the mind. And, of course, I never ever steered that course to an academic life *because* that is exactly what Dad would have wanted.

The questions continue.

'What is your biggest concern when putting on an event?'

'Fire' is the only answer. I can do everything I can to get us past Health and Safety and to a place where you have done anything in human nature to be compliant but you can't legislate for 150 tables with lit candles in a marquee and the whole thing going up in smoke. Candle paperwork can generally be at least three pages long – just for candles!

I make sure that I personally position all the fire extinguishers and if my capacity is over 1000 people always book the St. Johns Ambulance crew.

'You say you have not had disasters, but what are the greatest challenges?'

There comes the smart follow up question.

No question. Health and Safety. Security.

Health and Safety is a very unique category because it almost needs foul play or disaster before new legislation arrives. That is to say that generally, you only learn from mistakes – after it has gone wrong.

But, without a shadow of a doubt, it is also bred on *insecurity* so even a paperclip is covered off and that comes down to one thing. Nobody wants to get sued.

Disabled toilets and ramps, the weight of the stage and the steps up to it. All of this is now standard. Getting into Manchester United is about 300 pages worth of sign-off, though of course, when I am in, I am allowed to park in the Directors' car park. Obviously!

Staffing lists are a nightmare if you are at the Palace. I can't control it if one of my guys thinks he is Rudolf Nureyev on top of the ladder, falls off and is rushed to hospital. That happened. But it does leave me a bloody nightmare trying to get a new name on the cleared list. In the end, you have to bullshit your way in.

Never rule out nature either – and I don't mean the weather. At one event, a fox came in overnight and destroyed 50% of my marquee. Add foxes to your Health and Safety checklist!

And then from insecurity comes traditional security itself and this is an issue on the rise because of some of the places I

215

have to work in and some of the cultures amongst my clientele. Of course, there is also the paranoia amidst celebrities and that can be anything from paparazzi shots to gun shots.

Sometimes, I am dealing with characters who are licensed to carry weapons. At some events, they often put on their own security but even then, if I have 1000 people attending, I will have at least 60 staff and they need to be cleared (and safe)...as well obviously as having their own facilities to prepare, rest and eat in.

Then there is the law itself.

I have hosted quite a few bar mitzvahs where the parents have felt it was part of the night to take alcohol from behind the bar for thirteen year olds. When I see that, I stop the party. As soon as you have witnessed a child on the cusp of adulthood being taken away in an ambulance from such an event, there is no turning back – and I have seen that.

At one wedding, I was faced with two warring families. There is nothing worse and you just want the day over – both parties unable to lay aside their differences and neither really speaking to each other. Heaven only knows what the future held for the bride and groom!

The families could not have stood physically further apart on the day – the distance representing the huge gulf between them. You just want to do a good job, remain in control and get the hell out of there, knowing that it could kick off at any point.

Sure enough, I am asked to turn the music down by one of the groom's guests!!! A small issue like that, at a party for heaven's sake.

'Certainly, Sir,' I smile my reply.

I ignore him.

Then he summons me back, raising his hand and wiggling his finger at me. That is the kiss of death.

'What is this meat?' he asks very loudly in an attempt to humiliate me in front of the other eleven table guests.

'It tastes like dog meat,' he shouts.

I have to stay in control. But also, don't be rude to me:

'If you bark, Sir then you know it is,' I answer and turn away to see everybody's faces covered with their hands.

I didn't hear from him again that day. Point made, and indeed taken.

For 'magazine' weddings, the onus changes but the 'security' issues over privacy fall between the client and the publisher. Generally though, everybody's phone goes into a plastic bag with an ID number on it and they get it back at the end. That is how the *OK!* weddings manage to deliver. Grim – I know that on a couple's big day, you have to search all the guests but that is the deal. It makes for a better event in many ways because people do not know what to do with themselves without their mobiles – even at a wedding.

I will usually be allowed to take my own official photographer along on the proviso that I don't release any images within the first month of publication. Normally too, the magazines are not going to be taking every second cousin or hanger-on. There is a grey area which falls between a charity celebrity event where the public have paid to support the event and bought a table. You can understand why those people might have an issue here.

The length it takes to answer the question is the testament to how the game has changed and also a reality check to the lack of glamour in providing to the glamorous.

'Have you ever done an event for Number 10?'

One question inspires another…

'David Cameron, 2015, the Chinese Premier, Manchester Town Hall…next?'

'Have you ever had a legal letter after an event?'

I tell them that we put on a *Strictly* Come Manchester United. Drafted in all the big names from the show from Ola to Peter Schmeichel, from Charlotte Hawkins to Camilla Dallerup. A charity special.

It raised a lot of money.

The BBC write to me – very politely – to remind me about the trademark on the *Strictly* name.

I am sure I wasn't the first and won't be last. Every school nativity seems to work in an element of the hit show. Communities in the middle of nowhere put on replica evenings as they do *Manchester Has Got Talent* and The Great London Bake

Off. It would be impossible for them to litigate against all of these events and for the most part bad kudos. I wouldn't dream of infringing on someone else's brand rights as I would likely respond in the same manner if someone, for example, 'borrowed' my photos. The fact of the matter is that my *Strictly* was for a great cause, extended their brand without damaging it and the correspondence was very gentlemanly! I stress that I rarely pull tricks like this. You will understand that if you are organising a fundraiser with stars who collectively only have that show in common then you probably can't get them there, nor attract an audience unless under that umbrella.

I got away with it.

Sometimes it is easier to seek forgiveness than permission.

'What is the oddest rider?' shouts another from the back.

This is always a source of much fascination. This is the list of stars' demands to keep them happy backstage and generally turns out to be ignored by the talent when they turn up. The more B List the act, the more precocious the demands – one band whom you will have hardly ever heard of wanted blacked out vehicles in their pick-up vehicle, and 20 bottles of vodka. The bigger stars tend to be uber healthy requesting pine nuts and still water.

And then, of course, there is Diana Ross. A marquee event for a business mogul in the grounds of his estate. Obviously, we had to build a room with a shower and a bathroom in it plus provide an iron, an ironing board and somebody to iron – who was not allowed to look at her. Really…my icon destroyed by her own chain reaction!

'Would you ever do another reality TV show?'

You would never have got asked this question a few years ago but it seems to be some sort of credibility tick for the generation for whom *Big Brother* was a perfectly normal summer event!

'I got a call from *Real Housewives of Cheshire* and told them 100 K for one episode. They never called back.'

'Do you know the Real Housewives of Cheshire?' another would ask, laughing.

Of course, I do. I know everyone!

Being on that show though has some red flags. I felt that I was slightly burned in the edit when I did *The Millionaire Party Planner*. I risked becoming a parody if I repeated the experience.

I never wanted to be portrayed as *that type* of person. The story goes that one of them once turned up at the airport asking for an upgrade.

When rejected she gave them the 'do you know who I am?' line.

At which point, the check-in guy stood up and shouting down the long queue 'Excuse me, does anyone know who this lady is because she doesn't seem to?'

I couldn't endure such humiliation.

Funny, though!

Plus, of course, I tend to fly Business Class or private jet and people do know who I am!

That said, when I check into a hotel, I do always tell them to show me the third room first – that's because I will always reject the first room they offer me, and inevitably the next one too. By the time, they have taken me to the third choice, they are left with little choice but to give *me* an upgrade. Done with humour, candour, and chutzpah and making new friends who get you.

'How do you get everything to come together when you have to organise so many facets?'

A sensible question and the one I ask every time!

Apart from *years of experience* and trust in my team, the very simple answer to that lies in the recce.

If I am doing a gig on the third floor of The Hilton in Manchester, I know already before I have even lit a candle that I have one service lift. 500 people – the bands, the roadies, the caterers, the security, the lighting guys and hotel staff all fighting for one entrance point needs choreographing before you even choreograph the event. Know the logistics of the venue. That is one of my key rules.

On the day, we will all have comms on but I will take a separate channel so I don't hear all the responses of how I am doing everyone's head in. Obviously, I will be annoying people but that is what it takes.

'Where do you get your ideas from?' is a conference standard.

How do you actually even begin to answer that? Every party is different, yet each one takes inspiration from your knowledge of what has gone before or from inspiration such as the Diannes and Lorraines who you have worked with in the past. The needs of the hosts and their budget obviously drive it – plus current trends too. Who hasn't been asked to buy something from *Frozen* at some point in the last decade?

'What is the biggest budget you have ever worked to?

People get obsessed by the size of the money.

'£1.7 million,' normally blows any audience away.

You can hear the wows in the room every time. But this was the level we had got to.

And then I tell the story of the outdoor medieval fair and the bride with very eclectic tastes of German origin – her first marriage, his second and an entire weekend event. The challenge was to build an entire medieval world in the grounds of a hotel in the south of England, complete with actors and activities.

I understood what she was looking for and she gave me artistic license to let it flow. I built a white marquee with glass windows looking out onto the rolling hills of the countryside. The guests had to walk up eight steps to an elevated structure for the Saturday wedding party. Underneath it, I hid a medieval banquet for the following day. On the Saturday, nobody had any understanding of what lay beneath nor that the wonderful Sharleen Spiteri and her band Texas would be performing.

Every guest wore medieval dress.

That is a budget well spent!

Logistically, this is my best gig, my most challenging and my most exciting – and the crazier it gets, the more my staff respond. They know to come in with resolutions and not problems and we are all acutely aware that there is no rehearsal, nor a second chance on the day.

'Whose party would you most like to do?' is often thrown my way.

You never have a wish list. You wait and see who is at the end of the phone and occasionally tender for contracts.

In another era, I would have gone for Dean Martin, Sammy Davies Jnr, or Sinatra. I would have loved to have met Joan Rivers.

I draw the line at Elton John! I have to win and I think he would out diva me! Whilst, I have huge admiration for him, the vulnerable Liz would be worried that I wouldn't be good enough. Odd, I know, after all that we have done.

I look up once more towards the floor.

'I worked for you once at The Lowry Hotel.'

One of the students puts me on my guard.

I can handle most things and have heard most questions before but you can't know how this will go.

'Let me stop you right there,' I interrupt her to buy myself time.

'Was I rude to you?' I ask.

There is laughter all around, but they do not know that my insecurity and angst rise to the fore once again. I make no apologies for how I run my events – ruthlessly efficient without being ruthless per se. Clockwork is king.

I do know how other people perceive me. Especially in my new era.

I am well aware too that even though I have never met this person, she would have been part of a cog, if you like. That meant I was probably managing her boss on the day and that she was temporary contract staff and that might mean that she was somewhere at the end of the food chain whilst obviously being at the front of it serving.

I feel nervous.

'No, I was in awe of you,' she replies.

I am slightly taken aback.

Touched.

I realise she has come to hear me talk and specifically hunted out this seminar.

When we are done, a new process inevitably begins.

221

You rarely leave these events without someone nabbing you on the way out. I like that. The smart often hold back their questions for a little one to one on the way to the car park.

Then, the really smart get in touch with you. This is the new way. That is how I would have operated if I had been in the audience. It is not enough to show interest just once. If I have taught you anything in the hour-long session about networking, then you begin that path instantly by following it up with an email to me.

It doesn't mean that I hire you. But it means I remember you and then when you get back in touch the next time, you are more than entitled to begin with the words 'you might recall I wrote to you after...' and more than likely, I will and mentally file you away as smart and then the connection is made. I repeat, the second encounter can often be the key one. People rarely deal at stage one.

That is how I have worked and that is how networking works.

No surprise.

The girl from The Lowry emails:

'You inspired me,' she begins.

And I feel worth too.

We are poles apart in life experience and professional achievements. I take more from moments like this than almost any other. In the busy machine-like way in which you bash through your electronic correspondence at the start of every morning and relentlessly throughout the day, you rarely pause and read them again. People often say that in the digital era, one thing is absent in communication – you can't always convey tone.

I read her email twice and its message makes me glow all day. Not for ego, but for knowing that you made a difference, you set an example, you had treated people correctly even though you know what others say and for realising that mentoring was so valuable and on a two-way street. They learned from your experience and knowledge. You witnessed yourself in the mirror from decades before and for once liked what you saw.

It underlines to me that I want to do more and, more in front of the next generation. I could give them the blueprint on how to do what I do and yet nor would I want to spell it out. It is really important that they understand that you are going to make mistakes and those errors are part of making you successful.

Old school might have gone back to school, but I was the one who came out learning.

43 The Final Chapter

How to end my story? Well, they will lift the coffin and say 'How old, really? or 'She didn't look her age' or 'By God she was thin!' but in the meantime, much to the disappointment of some, I am still very much alive and kicking. In fact – better than that, I am very much back from the dead.

You have seen why.

I await the Amazon reviews.

'She loves herself.'

Clearly, I actually don't.

'She actually hates herself.'

Clearly, I don't either!

'What a name dropper.'

On the one hand – yes. On the other – impossible to tell my story without mentioning other people. I can't just call Prince William 'Bill' or Gary Barlow or Neville 'Gaz'.

It is essentially an ingredient of the narrative.

But yeah, it is a one hell of a world to be in at times and it is no different from turning up to a job interview with a CV. *Of course*, I am going to tell you about famous people who I have worked for. They breed my reputation and ensures further work. I simply cannot tell the story without dropping the names.

Perhaps, think about this?

What bits has she left out?

That is the smart question.

Omissions will be due to integrity or confidentiality on my part – but mostly age and a fading memory!

I hope you take something from the many elements in the preceding pages. You have a snapshot of old school Britain and those big companies offering management training schemes. You can see the rock'n'roll showbiz story but also the entrepreneurial spirit which is flourishing amongst so many people in the modern era.

At times, it must look like a great life. At others you perhaps see the ability to self-destruct.

I play the joker, act like a queen, and always have aces up my sleeve.

I can also collapse like a pack of cards.

A business brain in control, a heart often out of it.

A creative mind always at play.

Enchanted castles, a symbol of my work – a massive great drawbridge to cross to make dry land emotionally.

Blessed with beautiful children and adorable grand-children and surrounded by smart, diligent staff, I have finally arrived at a place marked peace and perspective.

I suspect there is a final chapter ahead.

As I write, Gary Neville calls to ask if I can get Howard Donald to DJ at his new hotel Stocks in Manchester.

A quick whatsapp and it's a yes!

For now, it has been a most unexpected wonderful rollercoaster of a ride.

And through it all I can tell you one thing.

The show will go on.

Except the show was about to grind to a colossal halt.

Which nobody saw coming.

I had written those final words in the Autumn of 2019. That was the end of my book. One eye on the future, and not so much about to take a leap of faith but more make a gentle transition towards my latest re-invention.

It seems a long time ago.

It is now 17 March 2020. My birthday lunch at the Ivy in Manchester. The usual shenanigans with my fellow Pisces celebrant Emma Neville, Antony Cotton and a few other close friends. Except it wasn't the usual debacle at all. There were a lot less people there than normal – and I am not talking about The Ivy. I refer to my party.

An undercurrent had set in. People were starting to show genuine fear. Yet, equally there was disbelief that it was actually real. Still, the over-riding emotion was 'it couldn't happen to me'.

Also – it couldn't happen *here*.

But it was. And it did.

If I say that it crept up on me and the UK then that suggests naivety and ignorance of a nation sleep-walking towards disaster. The truth is that is exactly what happened. It is well documented now that the Cheltenham Gold Cup hosted over a quarter of a million people and Liverpool's European match at Anfield against Atlético Madrid went ahead despite the Spanish team already having banned their own fans from attending their home games!

Later we learn that the initial strategy had been mooted as 'herd immunity' – a concept whereby it appears that if you throw everyone into the mix and there's a bit of illness in the air you build up your own system and defences against whatever may be lurking in the atmosphere.

Or as the Internet puts it:

'If enough people are resistant to the cause of a disease, such as a virus or bacteria, it has nowhere to go. While not every single individual may be immune, the group as a whole has protection'.

Yet, for a month we had seen pictures coming in on the TV news particularly from Italy. Old people were dying, the Venice Carnival in late February was abandoned hallway through and much of the North of the country had shut. At the same time, journalists were re-tracing their steps and locating the very first reports that had come out perhaps as early as the previous September (2019) from Wuhan Province in China.

They blamed the wet markets *or* said it had come out of a lab and was man-made.

Yet, by my birthday, Britain was still functioning but looking over its shoulder. I don't believe that it is a case that nobody was taking it seriously, more that nobody knew how serious it would become.

And then on 23 March 2020, like most of the nation, and in one of those rare coming-together moments, I turned on the telly.

45 Lockdown

There now follows a ministerial broadcast from the Prime Minister:

'The Coronavirus is the biggest threat this country has faced for decades and this country is not alone. All over the world we are seeing the devastating impact of this invisible killer and so tonight I want to update you on the latest steps we're taking to fight the disease and what you can do to help, and I want to begin by reminding you why the UK has been taking the approach that we have. Without a huge national effort to halt the growth of this virus there will come a moment when no health service in the world could possibly cope because there won't be enough ventilators and intensive care beds and doctors and nurses and as we've seen elsewhere in other countries that also have fantastic healthcare systems, that is the moment of real danger.

To put it simply if too many people become seriously unwell at one time, the NHS will be unable to handle it, meaning more people are likely to die not just from Coronavirus but from other illnesses as well so it's vital to slow the spread of the disease because that is the way we reduce the number of people needing hospital treatment at any one time so we can protect the NHS's ability to cope and save more lives and that's why we've been asking people to stay at home during this pandemic and the huge numbers are complying and I thank you all.

The time has now come for us all to do more. From this evening I must give the British people a very simple instruction: you must stay at home because the critical thing we must do is to stop the disease spreading between households. That is why people will only be allowed to leave their home for the following very limited purposes: shopping for basic necessities as infrequently as possible, one form of exercise a day...for example, they run, walk, cycle alone with members of your household...any medical need to provide care or to help a vulnerable person, and travelling to and from work but only where this is absolutely necessary and cannot be done from home.

That's all.

These are the only reasons you should leave your home. You should not be meeting friends. If your friends ask you to meet, you should say 'no'. You should not be meeting family members who do not live in your home; you should not be going shopping except for essentials like food and medicine, and you should do this as little as you can and use food delivery services where you can.

If you don't follow the rules the police will have the powers to enforce them including through fines and dispersing gatherings to ensure compliance with the government's instruction to stay at home. We will immediately close all shops selling non-essential goods including clothing and electronics stores and other premises including libraries, playgrounds and outdoor gyms and places of worship. We will stop all gatherings of more than two people in public excluding people you live with and will stop all social events including weddings, baptisms and other ceremonies but parks will remain open for exercise, but gatherings will be dispersed.

No prime minister wants to enact measures like this. I know the damage that this disruption is doing and will do to people's lives, to their businesses and to their jobs...'

Wow.

It was like an out of body experience.

I am never short of a word or two but sat there open-mouthed. This was truly jaw-dropping.

Boris Johnson promised that they would review the restrictions in three weeks' time and that there would be support ahead.

My muted birthday celebrations already seemed a distant memory. Nothing compared to this. You simply didn't have the tools to fight this war. We were about to put all our faith into something that we didn't understand. I was in a trance, vulnerability to the fore, alone but sharing this moment and these concerns with every other household in Britain.

I think he fell short of using the word that was now on everybody's lips – lockdown. But that was what it was.

The rumour mill had been in full force that afternoon. On a personal level, I did panic. I got my roots done immediately!

I remember thinking 'Thank God' that I had purchased the building where my office was. My focus immediately was on keeping the jobs of my staff. In time, one would take voluntary redundancy and this new word 'furlough' would become king. Everybody was saying that he was about to shut the country yet until you heard him say those words none of it seemed real. In my lifetime I had never known anything like it.

In an instant, it was as close to a wartime mentality on home soil that any of us could envisage. He didn't quite say the word 'rations' but that's the rhetoric he was using to describe the weekly shop. Loo rolls, you recall were at a premium. Certain items had a ceiling on how many you could purchase. He said you could exercise once a day which I found highly ironic that this would be many people's escape route for whom fitness had never been on the radar, but of course one particular phrase loomed large and bounced off the autocue and reverberated in my ears for the rest of the evening long after his six-minute speech had been consigned to TV archive history. In fact, this was already the televisual moment of the year.

For people in my game however, (i.e. self-employed, and in entertainment or hospitality) it became clear immediately we were somewhere down the pecking order. In reality, as you now know, we didn't even make the list at all. I had seen plenty in my business life including working through at least two recessions. This was off the scale. Immediately, I began doing sums in my head. There was a difference, of course, between the economy hitting the event industry when the national financial picture was on its knees such as in the credit crunch of 2007/8 but this was different. People did still trade back then; there was still work albeit budgets were tighter, and headcount was paramount.

Now, we simply weren't allowed to trade at all.

I couldn't know in the next 24 hours if the phone would ring off the hook or never ring again.

46 The Next Morning

There was an overwhelming amount of stuff to consider. The trick, of course though, was that we didn't know most of it at this point. One devastating number just kept staring back at me. I was about to lose a turnover of seven figures.

I just didn't know it.

I'm able to provide those numbers working backwards but remember, the day after the Prime Minister locked down the United Kingdom, most people clung to his notion that he would review the restrictions within three weeks. Indeed, the Premier League football programme was sending out exactly those signals...that this was a blip, a minor interruption. They even listed a restart date for April, re-scheduling fixtures that soon. The problem, as you know is that one day turned into another; a week became a month and here we are at the time of writing, one year on from the lockdown of 2020 and now facing an Indian variant of the virus.

Whilst there has been (certainly, initially) a collective attitude amongst so many people, standing on their doorsteps and clapping for the NHS, obviously it is human nature that one puts oneself first, especially as time wore on.

Did I have a business that would survive?

From my clients' point of view, each of them *are* individuals and require personal attention. Some had paid huge deposits, let alone the notion that their dreams were about to be shattered. And as that day did merge into a week and people soon realised that, despite the brief respite for the hospitality industry of the Help Out To Eat Out scheme, large scale events in the summer were off the menu. Many held out hope that there would be a Christmas hospitality season as usual, but even by late July when the pubs were open, the noises were not good. The first musings were the unlikelihood of the Manchester Christmas markets not taking place, and those came very early.

Remember that they open at the start of November and just like my game, require huge logistics, especially regarding transportation, suppliers and staffing. Many stallholders travel from abroad too. All the business around that focal point in the city centre clearly benefit too. There was also, as time wore on, that mixed emotion of weather indeed people would want to party like there was no tomorrow or never want to come out to play again.

It was inevitable that in that first 24 hours after the Prime Minister's announcement, many had their own self-interest at heart. The government were drawing up new legislation seemingly on a daily basis. Very few people had pandemic insurance, of course. In most public liability legal agreements there also existed the clause of force majeure (the notion that an act of God would nullify such claim.)

Now was not the time to include atheist in your personal details if you were looking to enforce that option!

It was in contracts for a reason. Now, you had to play that trump card.

Only time could really tell if this would be deemed the act of any deity…or devil. You can see therefore within 24 hours I am plunged into new legal terrain. You felt alone but everyone was in the same boat. It was how you responded that was going to count.

I did not panic in spite of the mayhem.

I did not let my mask drop, so to speak, whilst making sure I was wearing it all times.

Mayhem, on a global scale. There was a worldwide realisation that there was no immunity. This was not one of those occasions where you turned on the news about a war in Iraq and thought that even though we were involved it had little to do with me. It sent shock waves across the planet.

In a weird way, it was easier to deal with.

But I had to be ruthless.

The first question that many people asked me was 'Would they get their money back?'

I did not refund any deposits.

Some people threatened legal action.

'You're protecting your business, so am I,' I would tell them.

233

I had no choice, and I was not alone. The music industry is holding millions of pounds of advanced ticket sales in accounts for concerts that may not happen or might yet be rescheduled at dates against the convenience of the customer or for which the customer no longer has an appetite.

I don't therefore think my stance was unusual in our field. The travel industry, too. It is noted that it was quite slow to offer refunds with many, indeed, attempting to offer vouchers so that people held loyalty to that particular brand, and they at least held a cashflow. Futureproofing, they tend to call it nowadays.

In hindsight, I completely see that people were quite short-sighted in the advice that they were given, or they were not given any advice at all. That is quite understandable. Look at how the government continually made the rules up as they went along. Almost the only assistance that *I* could get from the Chancellor was the Business Interruption Loan. I cashed out to the max to protect myself. Choices were thin on the ground.

At night I would go to bed crying out of frustration.

I wasn't prepared to be defeated by a virus. By day, I would keep saying to myself that you have got to look after *you* despite the fact that I felt a moral responsibility to so many people who have been loyal exclusively to me over the years…florists, marquee builders, lightning crew etc…

Those relationships had been key. And would be so again.

One supplier said to me 'Liz, if the helicopter is going down, I want to be in it with you' but I knew now the real battle had begun.

It was just like in the 1980s starting out in business. The struggle to survive was once again underway and now having built this brand with my loyal staff and all of those contractors who were also on their knees, I soon found myself reduced to no staff at all.

I *did* relish the challenge and my gut feeling was that the longer the pandemic continued, the more assured I was that live events would return with a vengeance. I was adamant and indeed proved right that we would not see a live event until the summer of 2021! And that was as far as my crystal ball stretched! Having never borrowed a single penny in 30 years, I took absolutely everything available to ensure that I would be in the right place should that day arrive sooner rather than later. It seemed logical to me that there would be clear skies after the rainbow and in the darkest possible way those industries that were deprived such as travel, entertainment, and live music would surely return as the most sought after in demand activities. A boom was my gut feeling. As tough as it was to say, I sensed it was time to hold your nerve and ride it out. At the same time, I was forced to scale back my business.

It seemed very likely that this was the opportunity to move it in another direction. Those plans that I had mooted in what would have been the last couple of chapters of this book had to come to the surface now.

One theme shone through. My industry needed support. Everybody was looking for it. I received hundreds of emails, to which my standard reply was 'I'm afraid I don't have a crystal ball' but I did remain determined to focus on live events when that day would come. I felt that some of my competitors who were now setting up virtual events were not building a sustainable business model that would survive the pandemic. I didn't want to knee-jerk. I knew one thing: if you had a plan, you could still win.

I channelled my efforts therefore into my consultancy. I was my USP, and now was the time to navigate it.

Yes, I did have to compromise my expectations to secure clients, but the Golden Rule remained: brand is king.

People want that experience. We were all operating differently now but it didn't erase more three decades in the business. Some people say that everything happens for a reason. That may be true. What is clear is that in the history of mankind, evolution is a given. We have to adapt, and we have to change, and I say this, mindful of the sensitivities to those who have lost during this awful time: I know I'm not alone in voicing it, but the pandemic forced me to rethink my strategy at a time when I had been considering repositioning myself anyway.

Against that backdrop and with very little financial support in a creative industry that delivered dreams, many rivals joined together across the North West and the country and sought me out because of that very brand that I had built up.

I started to become a spokesperson. Magazines were very favourable to me. Television would call time and time again for a take on saving one of our most loved industries, and yes, it was an incredibly hard time personally. I know people who have passed away, I recognise the emotional and mental health toll on friends, colleagues, NHS staff and of course people who I will never meet. I was delivered a grandchild just two months before the pandemic began. Zoom aside, I have seen the little one just once…and briefly.

I believe this is what some people refer to as 'the new normal'. The truth of the matter is simple. There were opportunities aplenty but because of Covid, I have worked harder during the pandemic than at any other point in the last five years. Working from home means I go tougher at it. I also have better focus. Without this crisis, I would have been looking for that exit plan in my own surroundings.

It might not have come.

I feel confident in a business that always offers insecurity. It is true that I had *never* really realised the value of the cotton wool around me until this point. I sold the office building, and my desk at home became a Wicker basket. It resembled those early days of setting up in the toilet. I was never prepared to be influenced by negativity. Indeed, once the initial fear and uncertainty that accompanied the realisation that Britain was shut had passed, on a personal level forming the consultancy and to a small degree, starting again took the panic out of ageing.

Simply, the virus levelled everybody. However much money you've got, the technology we were now using had obviously changed but whilst the method was different, the rule remained the same:

It was still vital to meet people. Plus, there came the dawning realisation of 'why haven't we done this sooner?' The amount of time and money saved in working from home was extraordinary. I could, on some days, have completed five Zooms in the time it would have taken me to commute to Manchester and back home.

These are important points.

All of us had exactly the same skills that we had before the Prime Minister spoke to the nation. For some the shock of what was incoming numbed our own self-worth. Once I had dusted myself down, I knew I had the armoury to bring to other businesses the consultancy that perhaps initially was more of a hobby but manifested itself into something that a lot of brands were craving.

Everybody was desperate for support.

Often in life, we undervalue ourselves. The crushing effect of the pandemic would be a legitimate reason for a nation to do so en masse. Once I had grasped what lay ahead, I was clear that I had collected valuable skills over a lifetime which people were still prepared to pay for. Indeed, in some cases more prepared to pay more for. The virus took me out of Narnia and removed me from my party box. I found new friends and clients in the chef Tom Kerridge and his Bull and Bear in Stocks Hotel Manchester. I consulted for the Ashley Estate, Victor Restaurants came calling and I began work as a mentor for

Broadway Insurance and an exciting and dynamic kosher catering business called Feast. The underlying truth is that people were still investing in longevity, reliability and reputation. Dare I say it, mindful of the pressures that the pandemic brought on all sectors of life, I learned a lesson that I would pass on to others:

I was enjoying myself more than ever and, reinvention albeit it born out of necessity, could happen overnight.

A word in your ear.

I am well aware that there is no such thing as an *overnight* success. You have to have done the hard years to effect that transformation so quickly. As mental health came to the fore and people rallied looking for answers, one other aspect was also clear. People wanted to talk.

You will probably recall the scenes before the government introduced the tier strategy ahead of finally imposing an extended lockdown in late 2020. Manchester and its Mayor Andy Burnham became particularly vocal as a North-South divide seem to rear its ugly head again. At the heart of much of the rhetoric was indeed the entertainment industry. The North West did seem to have a voice that united the sector.

Obviously, I don't watch news all day long but I am not really aware of other regions in the country banging the drums (so to speak) for live music, nightclubs, restaurants and outdoor events in the brief period in the summer of 2020 before that grim autumn. London, you may recall was largely open and nothing accentuated this more than going from a Tier Two to Tier Four status in a matter of hours over one weekend.

I did resort back to Plan A when it looked as though there was a brief window of opportunity midway through 2020. That is to say that the Ashley Estate wanted ways of waking up their property. I devised Tatton Social with food and drinks vans, market sellers and a fairground. In preparation for the event of course, I couldn't know if it could get pulled at any moment even though by the summer it did look like the country was heading back towards a more even footing (albeit prematurely.) Sadly, that was the only event I have been able to champion in the flesh during the pandemic and I didn't, as a policy, want to invest in something short-term just to survive Covid.

238

The need to talk *was* vital. You will note, for example, that for the first time in our lives we have regular government briefings that are watched by many as though they are mainstream television. In the changing landscape, the government understood it had to keep communicating even if sometimes made a mess of it. Mental health would clearly be the legacy post pandemic. I, too, wanted to see if I had the skills to cut it in the world of conversation outside of business deals and small talk.

I began to podcast in the late spring of 2020. I had debuted 'Events That Made Me' and, of course, enlisted many of the usual suspects from Ruth Langsford to talent manager Jonathan Shalit, Arlene Phillips and Gok Wan. I had never met Arlene, nor Gok Wan, but with my relentless perseverance I got their personal emails and invited them! They could always decline – but they didn't – and now I count them amongst my friends.

It was clear to me that, in building a new brand in the form of the consultancy, there was as much worth in creating your own media to generate genuine media opportunities. *Steph's Packed Lunch*, the new Channel 4 show hosted by Steph McGovern invited me to do a piece on weddings in lockdown. Next, I invented a Wicker basket cocktail for a Covid diamond wedding, and later as the first anniversary of the pandemic approached, I knew my strategy had been correct.

My own media made *the* media. One of my podcast guests was Howard Donald from Take That. *The Mirror* decided to run the tale of Howard's apparent dislike of some of the band's tracks! The show hit the Top Ten in Apple podcasts.

Wow.

Howard has always been a delight but signed off by thanking me and saying it had been his greatest pleasure.

He didn't have to do that interview. He trusted me to talk to. Obviously that little black book was still working its magic.

To lose a year of my life at my age is precious but at least I did not lose my life. The pandemic has been a life-*shaper* not a lifesaver. The most important thing to understand was that everyone was in the same boat and for me I am in a better place than I was because I now know where I'm going whereas before I had just contemplated it.

I am grateful to the pandemic for that alone.

I function best when I'm professionally challenged. It becomes an aphrodisiac. That does not mean that I am power crazy or money-driven. It cuts across all aspects of my life as a human being and as an entrepreneur. The pandemic has engineered that change and yes, a sense of grounding bore fruit too.

I met up with Dianne for the first time in years. One morning, I woke with a very weird feeling. She *had* struggled during the pandemic, *her* priorities had changed. I don't know if we will work together again. You don't rule it in, nor do you rule it out but it was clear that we were still on the same page and we laughed about the property investment that we made together which I got rid of for £265,000 that had netted her £4.2 million!

That return on the property is the sort of thing that you can hold resentment over. We were both too long in the tooth to see it as anything other than amusement.

Admittedly, sometimes it takes time to pass or a major event to build those bridges again. Frankly, we should have done it sooner.

Lessons learned. And I finally realised that being set free from a toxic relationship was the best thing that could have happened to me.

It seems obvious to me that if you are reflecting on Coronavirus, you should transparently put your cards on the table.

But no, I did not have Covid.

I am fortunate that I have not been affected directly nor do I have parents in a home.

For many of us of course, those special occasions in the calendar are big wake-up calls. Christmas was particularly horrendous. I have been due to go to Barbados. My band had been booked to perform to a capacity of 220 people that was now reduced to an unknown figure. I chose not to go.

Often, I have been thinking 'just another month, just another month of this and it will be okay'. By the time you read this we will have passed the deadline that has been road-mapped as our exit strategy. Yet also, I have to keep an eye on the global situation. France's lockdowns are not in synch with ours and The Swan Band are largely based there. Within days of our route to liberation, I am scheduled to organise a wedding for 140 people at a boutique hotel which we have taken over exclusively. The bride, a victim of a wedding in Italy, (at the Ferragamo Villa where they withheld her substantial deposit) contacted me to enlist my help in arranging her special day in the UK. She will not lose any deposits if this is cancelled because it is my job to protect her.

The phone has not stopped ringing.

Of course, there is a backlog too.

It is important to stress as well that you need simply more than 52 Saturdays in a year to get married on if that is still your chosen day to exchange vows.

The events that I have shaped normally take a fortnight's worth of construction at an exclusive venue, followed by an extensive derigging process. Therefore, some can take two to three weeks out of a calendar. If you want your dream wedding three years from now, you need to get to work!

That may well drive the market value of the product up as I intimated before. When hospitality returns in anything other than a stop-start capacity, it surely has to go through the roof. That feels logical.

However, there are many question marks ahead for the attitudes in organising such an event and indeed for attending it. How do we party in the future? Is it classy and respectful to once again invite Cinderella to the ball or if you were putting on an event for employees, would they simply rather have the money for the next few years rather than splashing on a night of excess? Many people have a lot to pay back. Everybody will remember this time in Covid.

I suspect restaurants will have a field day – those who have managed to avoid throwing in the towel. There is now nobody who has not missed a birthday. Many have seen anniversaries, graduations and christenings pass. From an organisers' point of view, you have to be very clear. Blame distribution lies ahead more than ever. If you think that Health and Safety has been a problem in the last couple of decades, wait until you come out of a pandemic.

I have always walked away at the risk of compromising myself but in the future, we may well be faced with attendees at a party having to show the so-called vaccination passport or indeed take a test that reads negative. These may, in the short term or forever, become an integral part of the event for both guests and suppliers. The onus for the health of the guests must fall on the client. The event planner of course, will have even tougher health and safety demands to be pandemic-compliant.

This will mean that insurance policies will skyrocket. For the first time, all businesses, whether in hospitality or otherwise, are taking seriously the concept that pandemics may start again or be with us in some guise forever. Against that backdrop, life has to get back to some sort of *normal*. We won't be using the phrase 'the new normal' anymore. It will just be what normal is but there will be a moment where we make a run for it and come back fighting and I suspect other occasions where we have to retreat once more.

Much of what happened has happened *will* stay with us. Lessons learned will mould us rather than destroy us. I can tell you that there isn't one moment where I allowed myself to wake up thinking that I haven't got a business despite those early days when I sobbed myself to sleep. I have taught myself time and time again to pick up the pieces. This is no different. In the shortest period of time, I witnessed the phone ringing off the hook to not ringing at all and then life becoming wonderfully chaotic all over again. I am engrossed in other challenges now into which I would not have evolved without this collective experience.

I remain a car crash, personally.

Professionally, I don't know how it would have been possible to have foreseen this as something beneficial but my own reinvention would not have come without my hand being forced, from building bridges to sharing fears and knowledge within the industry; from pausing to take stock of life in general, to understanding that there is another way to work-life balance.

In a world of Zoom, I have now finally been able to do a software update on my own self and re-booted the machine.

Let's get that party started.

Lightning Source UK Ltd.
Milton Keynes UK
UKHW020837030921
389959UK00001B/18